A Field of La..ₒ

ANTHONY ASTBURY is the director of the Greville Press, which he founded in 1975. He has published four collections of his own verse, edited selections and anthologies, including *The Tenth Muse* (Carcanet 2005), and written memoirs of his friends George Barker, W.S. Graham, John Heath-Stubbs, Harold Pinter and David Wright.

GREY GOWRIE is a poet, and has had a career as an academic, a company chairman, a Cabinet minister, Chairman of the Arts Council of England and Provost of the Royal College of Art. His collection *Third Day* (Carcanet 2008) was a Poetry Book Society Recommendation. He is a Fellow of the Royal Society of Literature.

Also available from Carcanet Press

The Tenth Muse: An Anthology
Edited by Anthony Astbury, with a preface by Michael Schmidt

Grey Gowrie
Third Day: New and Selected Poems

A Field of Large Desires

A Greville Press Anthology

1975–2010

Edited by Anthony Astbury
With a preface by Grey Gowrie

Man's youth it is a field of large desires,
Which pleas'd within, doth all without them please,
For in this love of men live those sweet fires,
That kindle worth and kindness unto praise,
*   And where self-love most from her selfness gives,*
*   Man greatest in himself, and others lives.*

Fulke Greville

CARCANET

in association with
the Greville Press

For the poets

First published in Great Britain in 2010 by
Carcanet Press Limited
Alliance House
Cross Street
Manchester M2 7AQ

Selection copyright © Anthony Astbury 2010
Preface copyright © Grey Gowrie 2010

Acknowledgements of permission to reprint in-copyright material can be
found on pp. 213–18 and constitute an extension of the copyright page.

The right of Anthony Astbury to be identified as the editor of this work
has been asserted by him in accordance with the
Copyright, Designs and Patents Act of 1988
All rights reserved

A CIP catalogue record for this book is available from the British Library

ISBN 978 1 84777 050 9

The publisher acknowledges financial assistance from Arts Council England

Typeset by XL Publishing Services, Tiverton
Printed and bound in England by SRP Ltd, Exeter

CONTENTS

PREFACE

This anthology celebrates two men from the town of Warwick, in the middle of middle England, four centuries dividing them. Fulke Greville was a friend and biographer of Sir Philip Sidney. He was a courtier, what we would term a senior civil servant, to Elizabeth the First and her successor James. Greville's long and successful career was crowned by the peerage of Brooke (later Brookes became revived Earls of Warwick) and, better still, tenure of the magnificent castle at Warwick. He was a poet, a good one, whom C.S. Lewis called a master of the plain style. He died early in the reign of Charles the First, in 1628. He is buried in a magnificent tomb in St Mary's Church in Warwick, a building as fine in its own way as Warwick Castle itself.

A few yards from St Mary's lives another poet, Anthony Astbury, now in his sixties. He is a master of very short, aphoristic poems. You expect such verses to be comical, witty. Astbury's best work is filled with heartbreak and longing. He taught for many years at a now vanished private school just outside Warwick. He is an elegant, dandiacal, rather iconic figure for the town he has inhabited more than forty years. He is single; a lover of women; a drinker of stout. He was a good tennis player and remains a keen student of tennis style and expertise. He knows the birth and burial places of English poets better than anyone living and makes cheerful secular pilgrimages to them quite regularly. He founded the Greville Press in 1975.

The Greville Press publishes poets living and dead in pamphlet form. Poetry is a visual as well as an aural art; it delights the mind's eye as well as the mind's ear. You respond best to poems when they look good and when you learn that they do not require translating into prose. A poem is its own kind of linguistic and communicative construct: it is possible to admire birds and dogs without confusing them. Poems are best read, therefore, singly or with but few of their fellows. The great collections of great poets are useful for reference but hell to read. A slim vol is okay; a pamphlet best of all. Astbury is a scrupulous proof-reader who loves verse. He is not a press man, a printer. The Greville Press has been fortunate over many years by being associated with such gifted printing press men as Robin Skelton, Peter Lloyd, Bryan

Foster, Martin Farren and Charlie Boxer. It is both pleasant and practical for this Carcanet selection from the pamphlets to appear, and it is an appropriate thank-you to Tony. But I hope that those who enjoy the anthology will seek out pamphlets past and to come. They sharpen the pleasure and the concentration offered by the poems themselves.

In his great essay *The Voice of Poetry in the Conversation of Mankind* (1950), the political philosopher Michael Oakeshott (a Greville Press fan) analyses the practical or day-to-day implications of thinking about human society in terms of discourse: conversation not assertion; language used to delight rather than argue. *A Field of Large Desires*, in Fulke Greville's own lovely phrase, beckons us to such abundance and difference. It is a field tilled out of friendship. Anthony Astbury was close to two poets, dead now but not gone, George Barker and W.S. Graham.

> It was because I was given the privilege of their friendship that I decided to start the Greville Press – simply to publish them. Little did I know that I would not be able to stop. I made a point of regularly checking to see which poets of the past and present were out of print and resolving, if they were, to do something about it.

In our society, poets are divided, too crudely, between those who are 'taught' in the schools and those who are not. The latter do get published but seldom remain in print for very long; recent technological innovations may improve things. The inverted commas emphasise Astbury's own belief as a teacher, which I share, that you need to read poetry and learn it by heart rather than deconstruct or decode it. Again, poetry is a special way of looking at the world; a bird not a dog. For all the elegance and understated modesty of the pamphlets, the Greville Press has done great service to literature. Many fine writers have been brought out of hiding. The list of contents of *A Field of Large Desires* is highly eclectic. Poems have been included because Astbury likes them and believes their makers are worth celebrating. As a host he can be stern but he is never snobbish.

'It must give pleasure', wrote Wallace Stevens of modern art generally. As the appended List of Greville Press Pamphlets 1975-2010 shows, I am not at all a disinterested reader. I published a collection with Oxford University Press in 1972; fell silent; was catapulted back into the arena by the Greville Press and the magazine *Agenda* in 2005. A miraculous effect of the Greville Press is that if Tony approves of you, your pamphlet rubs shoulders with your superiors. And you in turn make discoveries. Poems unknown to me, as various as Elizabeth Smart's 'Slightly Rhyming Verses for Jeff Bernard's Fiftieth Birthday' or B.H. Fraser's City of London poem 'Business Centre' or Arthur Osborne's version of Baudelaire's 'The Voyage' (interesting to compare with Robert Lowell's), have been a revelation as well as a pleasure. So are poems revisited: a Dowson, Crane's 'Episode of Hands', Alan Ross's 'Leave Train'. The only poems here reprinted which were not published by the Greville Press are those written by the founder. Their appearance is my fee for this Preface. Anthony Astbury has run a great press for nearly forty years against incalculable financial odds. He is a true *servus servorum dei*, a Sherpa on Mount Parnassus. Look, listen and say. Let all your conscious and less conscious faculties go to work. They will enjoy doing so and they too will enlarge.

Grey Gowrie

A FIELD OF LARGE DESIRES

Olive Tree

And so we sat the world's children,
Listening to the stately voices
Of history and tradition.
While words made an enemy of innocence,
The wise ones told,
How our heroes and martyrs had died,
So that we may be allowed our freedom
Under the still wiser ones.

Now we look through bright private windows,
At the stained glass scene,
And feel betrayed by the bound and stamped books
That committees set before us.

We shape the process through the dark
Thoroughfares of mind and soul,
Till finally we emerge to find
Only a Christmas and an Easter
To remind us
That somewhere high on a green hill,
A white cottage gleams,
And an old woman sits quietly under an olive tree,
Waiting for all her sons to come home.

GILLIAN ALLNUTT

from *Lizzie Siddall: Her Journal (1862)*

'Laudanum'

Laudanum
is half
a honeymoon – and by my little window blows laburnum,
morning brief

euphoria, the hour of butter
milk. But then the windblown
waterlight withdraws. The long dour
afternoon

grows over me, a hood, a close brown pod
and I –
my soul, my sun, my seed –
am poisoned inly.

'I, Lizzie, once a girl'

I, Lizzie, once a girl
growing up in the Old Kent Road,
give my soul
to God

the ironmonger.
Send word
to my father
when I am dead.

On a Dolphin

No more in delightful chase through buoyant seas
Shall I toss up my throat from the depths, nor blow around
The ornamented beak of the ship, exulting
In the carved figurehead, my image. But the sea's
Glittering blue has thronged me out of the moist element:
I lie stretched out on a narrow space of dry land.

'Many times lamenting, Cleina, the mother'

Many times lamenting, Cleina, the mother,
Has cried aloud on the tombstone of her girl –
She who died early – calling back her darling,
The soul of Philaenis, who, before her wedding,
Passed over the pale flood of the river of Death.

'In life this man was Manes, a slave'

In life this man was Manes, a slave:
Dead now, he passes as the equal of great Darius.

Translated by Carol Whiteside and John Heath-Stubbs

Zone

In the end you are tired of that world of antiquity

O Eiffel Tower shepherdess the bridges this morning are a bleating
flock

You have had enough of living in Greek and Roman antiquity

Here even the motorcars look like antiques
Only religion is still quite new religion
Remains as simple as the airfield hangars

You alone in Europe O Christianity are not ancient
And the most modern European is you Pope Pius X
But shame restrains you whom the windows watch
From going into a church and confessing this morning
You read handbills catalogues posters singing aloud
That's what poetry is this morning and for prose there are the papers
There are 25 centime instalments full of detective stories
Portraits of the famous and a thousand assorted titles

This morning I saw a pretty street whose name I forget
It was the bright new herald of the sun
Directors and labourers and beautiful shorthand-typists
Pass through it four times a day between Monday morning and
Saturday evening
There each morning the siren wails in groups of three blasts
An irascible bell in full cry sounds towards noon
And the signwriting and the writing on the walls
And the nameplates and the notices shriek like parrots
I love the gracefulness of this factory street
Which is situated in Paris between the Rue Aumont-
Thiéville and the Avenue des Ternes

And look what a young street it is why you are only a small child yet
Your mother dresses you only in blue and white

You are very pious too and like your oldest playmate René Dalize
You love nothing so much as the ceremonies of the Church
At nine o'clock the gas is turned down so low it burns blue and you
                                        slip out of the dormitory
To pray all night in the school chapel
While the eternal adorable amethyst depths
The blazing glory of Christ revolves forever
It is the lovely lily we all nurture
The redhaired torch the wind cannot put out
The pale and rosecoloured son of the dolorous mother
The evergreen tree of all prayers
The intertwined stems of honour and eternity
The sixpointed star
It is God who dies on Friday and is resurrected on Sunday
Christ climbing heavenward faster than aviators
Holder of the world altitude record

Apple of Christ's eye
His twentieth pupil of centuries makes progress
And changed into a bird this century soars like Jesus
The demons in the abysses raise their heads to look at it
They say it imitates Simon Magus of Judaea
They cry out even if it can fly it's only a fly-by-night
But the angels flutter about this bonny flier
Icarus Enoch Elijah and Apollonius of Tyana
Hover about the first aeroplane
Dividing from time to time to make way for those who are exalted
                                        by the Holy Eucharist
Those priests eternally ascending raising the Host
And at last the aeroplane comes down without folding its wings
And then the sky fills with millions of swallows
Crows and falcons and owls come winging
Ibis and flamingoes and marabou storks out of Africa
The Roc celebrated in fable and by poets
Glides clutching Adam's head in its talons the first head of all
From the far horizon the eagle swoops uttering a great cry
And the small hummingbird comes from as far as America
And the long and sinuous pi-his come from China
They that have only one wing and fly by couples
And then the Dove the Immaculate Spirit appears
Escorted by the lyre bird and the eyed peacock
And the phoenix the self-engendering pyre

Veils everything for an instant with its burning ashes
The sirens leave the perilous passages of the sea
And arrive singing all three of them most marvellously
And all of them eagle phoenix and Chinese pi-his
Fraternize with the flying machine

And now you are walking all alone in Paris among the crowds
And herds of roaring omnibuses are rolling past you
The anxiety of your love clutches at your throat
As if you were never going to be loved again
If you lived in the old days you would enter a monastery
You feel ashamed when you catch yourself saying a prayer
You laugh at yourself and your laughter crackles like hellfire
The sparks of your laughter light up the depths of your existence
Like a picture hung up in a gloomy museum
And sometimes you go up close to it and look at it

Today you are walking in Paris and the women are covered with
blood
This was and I wish I could forget it it was at the time of the failing
of beauty

Surrounded by a fervency of flames Our Lady looked at me in Chartres
And in Montmartre the blood of your Sacred Heart drowned me
I am sick of hearing the blessed words
And the love from which I suffer is a shameful disease
And the image of you persists through anguish and insomnia
And when I am near you this image always passes away

Now you are by the shores of the Mediterranean
Under the lemon trees which flower from year's end to year's end
You go for a sail with your friends
And one of them is a Nicean and one is a Mentonian and there are
two Turbiasques
We look down in horror at the squids of the deep
And through the seaweeds Christ's fishes are swimming

You are in a garden in the suburbs of Prague
You feel very happy and there is a rose on the table
And instead of writing your prose story you look at the metallic
Sheen of the beetle asleep in the heart of the rose

Terrified you see yourself depicted in the agates of Saint Vitus
You were as sad as death the day you saw yourself there
You are like Lazarus driven mad by daylight
The hands of the clock in the Jewish quarter are turning backwards
And you are passing slowly backward through the history of your life
Climbing the hill to the Hradchin and listening in the evening
To Czech songs being sung in the taverns

Here you are in Marseille among the watermelons

Here you are in Koblenz at the Sign of the Giant

And here you are in Rome under a Japanese medlar tree

Here you are in Amsterdam with a girl whom you think beautiful
                                              and who is ugly
She is supposed to be marrying a student from Leyden
Where they let rooms in Latin CUBICULA LOCANDA
I remember it I spent three days there and as many at Gouda

Now you are in Paris at the Examining Magistrate's
They have placed you under arrest like a criminal

You made painful and joyful journeys
Before you discovered falsehood and old age
You suffered love at twenty years old and at thirty
I have lived like an idiot and wasted my time
You no longer dare look at your hands and every minute I feel like
                                                            sobbing
Over you over the girl I love and over everything that has terrified you

You are looking at the eyes of those emigrants which are brimming
                                                        with tears
They believe in God they pray the women suckle their children
They fill the waiting room at the Gare St Lazare with their odour
They trust in their stars as the three wise men did in their star
They hope to make money in the Argentine
And go back to their own country with a fortune
One family carries an eiderdown with it as you carry your heart
This eiderdown and our dreams are equally unreal
Some of the refugees stay here and take rooms
In the Rue des Rosiers or the Rue des Écouffes in hovels

I have often seen them taking the air in the street in the evening
They move as slowly as pieces in a game of chess
Above all there are the Jews whose women wear wigs
And sit bloodlessly in the backs of their shops

You are standing in front of the counter in a low drinking place
Drinking a penny coffee among the unfortunates

You are in a great restaurant at night

Those women are not evil but still they have their troubles
Each one of them has made her lover suffer even the ugliest

Who by the way is the daughter of a policeman in Jersey

Her hands which I hadn't noticed before are hard and calloused

I feel a great pity for the scars on her belly

Now I make a humble face for a poor girl with a horrible laugh

You are alone and soon it will be morning
Milkmen are banging their churns in the streets

Night passes away like Métive the Beautiful
Like Ferdine the False like Leah the Forlorn

And you are drinking spirits that burn your mouth as your life burns it
Your life that you toss off as though it were a glass of spirits

You are walking towards Auteuil you wish to go home on foot
To sleep among your South Sea Island fetishes and West African idols
Which are Christs of dissimilar forms and of other beliefs
Minor Christs of obscurer longings

Farewell Farewell

Beheaded sun

Translated by Oliver Bernard

Woman

When the alimony don't arrive
or the giro from The Social,
when he gets in drunk,
or worse, he's sober and guilty,
I wonder why
I let things get this bad.

When my pal, Val, who lives next door,
says I'm a bore, a nag, or was it a slag?
and she weren't surprised he'd buggered off,
only amazed he hadn't done it before,
I wonder what
sort of a monster I've become.

When the woman from The Welfare
says the kids will 'go into care'
if I don't stop them glue sniffing
and behaving like hooligans,
I wonder how
I can live with my despair.

When the letter full of longwords
says the money's cut off
'Due to cohabitation'
(information from the neighbourhood sewer)
I wonder where
I can feed my hungry heart.

When the HP for the tele's overdue
(and so is my monthly period)
and there's no money for the meter,
I just don't know what to do.
I wonder whether
being white would make life easier.

Gargoyle

The gargoyle crept
with cloistered wings
from the decaying roof
through the spider's web
of skeletal scaffolding
and waited.

The flying buttress,
paralysed for a hundred years,
since his poison had found its mark,
endured his soiled water vomit
with the acid rain bile
and watched.

The pigeons paused
in their geriatric mumbling,
unknown instincts pulsing
through dappled grey down
so that they whimpered
and shuddered.

The girl-child crossed
the church courtyard where
the sundial said no time,
curtsied to pick
a fireflower from the flagstones
and smiled.

The gargoyle uncoiled
gryphon clawed hands
from testicle pockets,
chiselled the crumbling cement
from under the cornerstone
and pushed.

Sex Objects

It is said that
nothing so becomes a man
as gentleness and humility

but big balls
in a cross-your-crotch jockstrap
lift me up

and necks like tree trunks
touched by soft hair tendrils
draw my sap

and small buttocks
inside tight trouser chrysalises
fuel my fantasies.

ANTHONY ASTBURY

Letter

Dear ——,

You drink too much
for your own good.
Pull yourself
together
before it's too late.
Stop smoking.
Get out of debt.
For God's sake
what's going to
happen to you?

Look! I sympathize.
You'll get over it.
She's only a woman!
And remember
poetry's okay
as a *hobby*.
In other words
grow up –
and settle down.

Love, Bonkers.

Warwick

What are they doing to you Warwick?
Surely not trying to change you
The fathers of the vandals in the park
Dreaming of inner relief roads?

Loss

I miss her from her top to her toes.
Awake, I dream I'm not alone.
Asleep, my hands are on a telephone.
Like night and day she comes. And goes.

English Lesson

Dreamer turned schoolmaster.

Boris Pasternak

The wear and tear within had been frightful,
Not easily measured and escorted back
To one whose only wish was to bring to life
A stranger; and in return accept a future
Standing before a class of boys
Ignorant of a troubled story being retold.

Warwick, 1966

GEORGE BARKER

Roman Poem III

A Sparrow's Feather

There was this empty birdcage in the garden.
    And in it, to amuse myself, I had hung
pseudo-Oriental birds constructed of
    glass and tin bits and paper, that squeaked sadly
as the wind sometimes disturbed them. Suspended
    in melancholy disillusion they sang
of things that had never happened, and never
    could in that cage of artificial existence.
The twittering of these instruments lamenting
    their absent lives resembled threnodies
torn from a falling harp, till the cage filled with
    engineered regret like moonshining cobwebs
as these constructions grieved over not existing.
    The children fed them with flowers. A sudden gust

and without sound lifelessly one would die
    scattered in scraps like debris. The wire doors
always hung open, against their improbable
    transfiguration into, say, chaffinches
or even more colourful birds. Myself I found
    the whole game charming, let alone the children.
And then, one morning – I do not record a
    matter of cosmic proportions, I assure you,
not an event to flutter the Volscian dovecotes –
    there, askew among those constructed images
like a lost soul electing to die in Rome,
    its feverish eye transfixed, both wings fractured,
lay – I assure you, Catullus – a young sparrow.
    Not long for this world, so heavily breathing
one might have supposed this cage his destination
    after labouring past seas and holy skies
whence, death not being known there, he had flown.
    Of course, there was nothing to do. The children
brought breadcrumbs, brought water, brought tears in their
    eyes perhaps to restore him, that shivering panic
of useless feathers, that tongue-tied little gossip,
    that lying flyer. So there, among its gods
that moaned and whistled in a little wind,
    flapping their paper anatomies like windmills,
wheeling and bowing dutifully to the
    divine intervention of a child's forefinger,
there, at rest and at peace among its monstrous
    idols, the little bird died. And, for my part,
I hope the whole unimportant affair is
    quickly forgotten. The analogies are too trite.

Morning in Norfolk

        As it has for so long
        come wind and all weather
        the house glimmers among
        the mists of a little
        river that splinters, it

seems, a landscape of
winter dreams. In the far
fields stand a few
bare trees decorating
those mists like the fanned
patterns of Georgian
skylights. The home land
of any heart persists
there, suffused with
memories and mists not
quite concealing the
identities and lost
lives of those loved once
but loved most. They haunt it
still. To the watermeadows
that lie by the heart they
return as do flocks of swallows
to the fields they have known
and flickered and flown so
often and so unforgettably over.
What fish
play in the bright wishing
wells of your painted
stretches, O secret
untainted little Bure,
I could easily tell,
for would they not be
those flashing dashers
the sometimes glittering
presentiments, images
and idealizations
of what had to be?
The dawn has brightened the
shallows and shadows and
the Bure sidles and idles
through weed isles and fallen
willows, and under
Itteringham Mill, and
there is a kind of rain-
drenched flittering in the
air, the night swan still
sleeps in her wings and over it all

the dawn heaps up the hanging
fire of the day.

Fowell's tractor blusters
out of its shed and drags
a day's work, like a piled sled
behind it. The crimson
December morning brims over
Norfolk, turning
to burning Turner
this aqueous water colour
idyll that earlier gleamed
so green that it seemed
drowned. What further
sanction, what blessing
can the man of heart intercede for
than the supreme remission
of dawn? For then the mind
looking backward upon its
too sullied yesterday,
that rotting stack of
resolution and refuse,
reads in the rainbowed sky
a greater covenant,
the tremendous pronouncement:
the day forgives.

Holy the heart in
its proper occupation
praising and appraising this
godsend, the dawn.
Will you lift up your eyes
my blind spirit and see
such evidence of
forgiveness in the heavens
morning after golden
morning that even
the blind can see?

CHARLES BAUDELAIRE

Le Voyage

I

For the child enthralled by maps and picture books,
The universe is a vast appetite.
How limitless the world by lamplight looks!
How small it is when lit by memory's light!

One morning we set out, our brains on fire,
Hearts filled with bitter hopes and memories,
And the waves rock our infinite desire
On the cold cradle of the finite seas:

Some glad to leave a land of infamies,
And some the horrors of their youth; some still,
Astrologers drowned in a woman's eyes,
Strange-scented Circe of despotic will.

To escape the dread change into beasts, they drink
Deeply of burning skies and light and space.
The ice that gnaws them and the suns that shrink
Slowly remove the marks of her embrace.

But the true voyagers alone are they
Who go but for the going, light of heart;
Who from their destined courses never stray
But always, not knowing why, must say 'Let's start.'

Those whose desires like clouds forever range
Yearning, as martyrs for the heavenly throne,
For vast voluptuous pleasures, new and strange,
Whose names the human mind has never known.

II

In hideous mimicry, we dance and leap
Like tops and balls, forever tossed and spun
By Curiosity, even in our sleep,
As, whipped by a cruel Angel, spins the sun.

Strange situation, where the goal recedes,
And, being nowhere, can be every place,
Where man, whose hopes are hardier than weeds,
Seeks rest in a perpetual mad chase.

The soul is like a battered ship that seeks
In vain its own Icaria. The relief
Shouts from the bridge 'Ahoy!' The look-out shrieks
'Love… glory… fortune!' Hell! We're on a reef!

And every island that the look-out spies
Is Eldorado, ours by destined right.
Anticipation, opening eager eyes,
Finds barren rocks in the cold morning light.

Poor lover of chimeric lands, alas,
What shall we do with him, confine or kill,
This drunk inventor of Americas,
Whose mirage makes the gulf more bitter still?

So might an old tramp, stumbling head in air
Through mud, dream of a brilliant paradise;
And candlelight in any sordid lair
Bring Capua before the wanderer's eyes.

III

Amazing travellers! What proud histories
We read in the deep oceans of your eyes.
Show us the treasures of your memories,
Those marvellous gems made of the seas and skies.

We wish to travel without sail or steam.
Divert us from the boredom of our prisons

By throwing on our minds, strained as a screen,
Your memories framed in faraway horizons.

Tell us, what have you seen?

IV

'The usual sights:
The stars, the waves, the sand and the sea foam.
In spite of all disasters, shocks and frights,
We were as often bored as here at home.

'The glory of the sun upon the violet sea,
The glory of cities as it sinks from sight,
Lit in our hearts a burning urgency
To plunge into the sky's reflected light.

'Cities and lands, however rich and proud,
Had never for us half the interest
That chance can give to any passing cloud;
And our desires robbed us of all rest.

'– Enjoyment of desire renews its force.
Desire, old tree manured by our delight,
While your bole thickens and your bark grows coarse,
Your boughs reach vainly towards the source of light.

'Will you grow forever, great tree, more tenacious
Than the cypress? – Meanwhile we have culled with care
Some sketches, my good friends, for your voracious
Scrap book, who think all things from far are fair.

'We've bowed before horned idols, and stood under
Gemmed thrones lit by their constellated gleams;
Carved palaces whose caves of magic plunder
Would fill your bankers with disastrous dreams;

'Dresses that drown the eyes in drunken bliss;
Women with coloured teeth and nails; all kinds
Of subtle jugglers whom the serpents kiss.'

V

And then, and then what else?

VI

'O childish minds!

'Lest we forget our miserable estate,
We've found, unsought, wherever we have been,
On every stage of the stairway of fate,
The eternal tedium of immortal sin.

'Woman, vile slave, who adores without disgust
Her stupid self, false, humourless and vain.
Man, greedy tyrant, mean, cruel, full of lust,
Slave of the slave, gutter without a drain;

'The hangman's laughter and the martyr's groan;
The blood that spices and perfumes the feasts;
The poison of power that eats away the throne;
The lash that leaves the multitude like beasts;

'Several religions, much like ours, that spread
Their spiders' webs towards heaven; and Sanctity,
Wallowing, like a weakling in a feather bed,
In whips and hair shirts for its lechery.

'Now and forever fools, Humanity,
Prattling away, surrounded by disaster,
And crying to God in outraged agony,
'I curse you, O my image and my master!'

'And the less dull, the devotees of Mania,
Fleeing the herd by Destiny penned in,
And sheltering in opium's vast arcana!
– Such is this world's eternal bulletin.'

VII

O bitter truth, learnt from all lands and races:
That the world's smallness and monotony
Is our unchanging image; an oasis
Of horror in a desert of ennui.

To set out or to stay? If you must, flee,
If you can, stay. One hides, another runs
To escape the sleepless deadly enemy
Time! Alas, one of those unresting ones,

Like the Apostles and the Wandering Jew,
And nothing helps, no ship or chariot,
To foil the fatal thrust; a very few
Can kill him without stirring from the cot.

And when at last his foot's laid on our spine, our
Hearts can still hope, and we'll still cry 'Away!'
As when of old we first set out for China,
Eyes on the sea, and hair blowing in the spray.

Upon the Sea of Shadows we'll embark,
And like an eager boy's our hearts will beat.
Hear the sad siren voices in the dark
Singing 'Come this way, you who wish to eat

'The perfumed Lotus! Here the harvest is
Of the strange fruits your hearts have hungered for.
Come, and drink deep of the oblivious bliss
Of an afternoon that lasts for evermore.'

And from the voice we recognize the spectre;
Our Pylades reach towards us from below.
'To refresh your heart, swim out to your Electra,'
Says she whose knees we kissed so long ago.

VIII

O Death! Old captain, let us re-embark.
This country bores us. Let us sail away.

Though sea and sky fade in the frigid dark,
Our hearts are burning like a tropic day.

Pour out the poison that we long to drink,
We thirst, our brains burn so, to plunge into
The deepest gulf, be it Heaven or Hell, and sink
To the depths of the Unknown for something new.

Translated by Arthur Osborne

WILLIAM BELL

'All summer long in dreams I would remember'

All summer long in dreams I would remember
an empty tower upon a northern shore
where evermore December and December
return, return, but we return no more;

there where you left a chamber swept and garnished,
there where the air should hold your fragrance still,
the floor is thick with dust, the mirror tarnished,
the paint is blistered on the windowsill.

All summer like the butterflies and bees
which beat against the dirty windowpane
my dreams within my heart have had no rest,

no rest, till from across the freezing seas
the storms, the storms are gathering once again:
– but why do you put your hand upon your breast?

'Perhaps the unbroken colt beside the river'

Perhaps the unbroken colt beside the river
whose clumsy power compels the rider's thigh
toward no lust to master as a lover,
but the offenceless love of mastery;

or else the cliff that tempts the climber's fingers
into a cold impossible caress;
perhaps these were the fierce desire that lingers
and fills my body with its restlessness;

for both the lifeless and the brute creation
gave to you of their power and their grace,
and it is their rejection that I feel:

for I can find no bridle to my passion,
no hold at all upon that hanging face,
oh most desired, since unattainable!

GIACONDA BELLI

New York

Forest of hurricanes
The city of the tall chimneys is approaching
It is New York
New York
The clouds get tangled up in the crest of the city
From above the streets resemble the grid
of an immense steel labyrinth
The dense smoke rises up the breath the steam
the foam of people who live
waves of human beings struggling in low tide and high tide

on the streetcoasts against the skyscraper rockpeaks
The plane speeds over smooth erect ramps
blue white bulbs mark out the runway
We descend to the city of tumults
knot of crowds
noise of trains buses taxis
innumerable faces
faces seen a single time
unrepeatable consumed in the depths
moving towards unknown destinations
suitcases labels evoking far-flung countries
we arrive at the same time at the line boarding yellow taxis
we separate without knowing who we are
all of us are going somewhere
without looking at each other
bodies crammed together bodies colliding
eyes that do not meet
We get in we race we plough through illuminated motorways
bridges arches the dark river flowing abandoned to its fate
like us
like everyone here archipelagos islands without bridges
crossing bridges ingeniously crafted in steel
New York
old sorceress fascinating changing chameleon
pandora's box open streets open skirts
open doors towards temptation
books furniture clothes magazines restaurants shops
shops shops expensive cheap cinemas theatres fashions
sports pornography shoes cheese ice cream
concerts opera boutiques huge stores
the largest store in the world
floors floors floors one on top of the other
cafeterias hamburgers supermarkets
salmon oysters avocados orange juice
machines to play with get turned on to think
to calculate drugs to dream with
headphones to glide along the streets listening to music
ploughing a path weaving in and out
absent from the street pedestrians passing by
New York
of tall twin buildings
the tallest in the world: the World Trade Building

the commercial building dominating the entire city
God of the city
two towers two eyes watching
Forest of hurricanes
So many concrete trees so many high windows
When the wind blows furious currents are created
enormous mouth blowing its own climate
blizzards stirred up by the skyscrapers
the wind trapped in this giant network
born of the hand of man
New York
here worked work thousands of people
they left leave behind their years their dreams
they begot beget children
they raised raise these cloud-catching columns
ports airports stations roads
planes trains boats brought Greeks Irish
Italians Chinese Indians Arabs Latinos Poles
Russians Japanese Filipinos Africans
seekers of fortunes fugitives slaves
exiles adventurers musicians poets
scientists madmen gangsters anonymous immigrants
waves of faces blurred dissolved lost
Here lives a people
a tree of many roots
lives deaths of those who here got along together
associates in solitude and deafening noise
New York
Central Park
The squirrels approach us
It's rare that they approach but I called them I spoke to them
They came timorously walking over the grass stiffened by the winter
Smooth trunks without leaves
naked skeletal beautiful in the cold late afternoon
Young people playing baseball couples embracing
we embracing merged in
strolling without faces without identity for anyone
grains of sand on the beach tumult of anonymity
Docks of New York
the river flowing the Hudson pouring out
stretching out its silver strip black oaks
silhouetted in the late afternoon the man walking his dogs

the homosexual phoning from a public booth
asking for his lover
rusty nails eaten away by the water
scratches of planes winding through the congested sky
thousands of planes all day arriving and departing
underground trains
thundering underground world rails stations
carriages painted with slogans that say nothing
graffiti on the walls unintelligible
signs of those who don't know what to say
merely that they want to say something confused
to leave a mark to attract attention armed
with cans of paint covering the aluminium with scrawls
running away from the police
raping murdering sirens around the clock
street fights insults hurled from anywhere
Faces alive dead happy sad
people who want to chat communicate with one another
talk among themselves the isolated ones
the woman screaming in the street
for God's sake help me – in Spanish –
passing by her no one stops
They go to their houses drink coffee
coffee morning noon and night
coffee brought from countries such as ours
tiny poor coffee exporting countries
countries that drink watery coffee so that in New York
we may go past shops where coffee saturates the smell of the entire
                                                                    street
New York
Fascinating old sorceress
Expensive whore sky high cost of living cost of food cost of books
cost of apartments
To enjoy yourself is to have money
You only need money
Without money you don't do a thing
Sacrosanct banks resembling confessionals
with code machines dispensers of money
you key in a number and notes come out
People go inside to withdraw their money
Standing next to each other respectfully
they don't exchange glances one would think they were praying

New York
Forest of hurricanes
Horrible beautiful city
poor rich people poor poor people
fascination bewitchment magic of abundance
waves of people struggling in high tide and low tide
happy misfortunate human beings
squeezed into this contractile womb
city vomiting them giving birth to them
people of all colours caged in pressing against each other
shunning each other's eyes running off to their little worlds
on the look-out struggling to avoid any mix-up over their names
their identity to recognise their window in the confusion of floors
not to lose their key house job wife man
tears touch semen
to survive
to survive like us who survive
who struggle to survive those who survive
New York
Forest of hurricanes

Tomorrow we will land in Augusto Cesar Sandino airport
and the route the runway the landing will be lit up with candles
hundreds of tiny poor candles.

Translated by John Lyons

The Unpredictable

The raw and overwhelming danger
Of the first grief and the first hunger,
Too much, I dare say, to be caught
By a child's heartbeat and his thought.

Mercifully, though, from too much violence
There is oblivion and silence,
Postponing love and the great anger,
For latter days when we are stronger.

But to go round and round again
In a dead dream of dead men,
From the stopped heart and the checked word;
This also has occurred,

And tall constructions from a first
Unquenched and undiminished thirst,
Out of weakness and much danger,
The laurel crown, the hero's posture.

To have suffered, though, to have done
With the black light of the first sun,
Though the drink's stale, the bread putrid,
This is beyond love and hatred;

To have worked out, to exceed
The Furies and the human need,
Is unpredictable, a grace
Of no time, no place.

An Epitaph

By much speaking I fled from silence,
To many friends from the one stranger,
By food and drink I cheated hunger,
And by meek words, abuse and violence.

My loss increased as I grew richer,
My load more great with lighter burden,
With less guilt, more sought I pardon.
As light flowered, I grew blinder.

I quenched my thirst by lack of water,
And found myself where I was absent,
Faith half I proved by the inconstant
Moon: truth because I was a liar.

Now far still from the heart's centre,
But with less storm, less crying,
I wait for birth again, now dying
Has opened its door and let me enter.

ROBERT BRIDGES

Triolet

When first we met we did not guess
That Love would prove so hard a master;
Of more than common friendliness
When first we met we did not guess.
Who could foretell this sore distress,
This irretrievable disaster
When first we met? – We did not guess
That Love would prove so hard a master.

EMILY BRONTË

'I am the only being whose doom'

I am the only being whose doom
No tongue would ask, no eye would mourn;
I never caused a thought of gloom,
A smile of joy, since I was born.

In secret pleasure, secret tears,
This changeful life has slipped away,
As friendless after eighteen years,
As lone as on my natal day.

There have been times I cannot hide,
There have been times when this was drear,
When my sad soul forgot its pride
And longed for one to love me here.

But those were in the early glow
Of feelings since subdued by care;
And they have died so long ago,
I hardly now believe they were.

First melted off the hope of youth,
Then fancy's rainbow fast withdrew;
And then experience told me truth
In mortal bosoms never grew.

'Twas grief enough to think mankind
All hollow, servile, insincere;
But worse to trust to my own mind
And find the same corruption there.

17 May 1839

A Visit to the Dead

I bought (I was too wealthy for my age)
A passage to the dead ones' habitat,
And learnt, under their tutelage,
To twitter like a bat

In imitation of their dialect.
Crudely I aped their subtle practices;
By instinct knew how to respect
Their strict observances.

The regions of the dead are small and pent,
Their movements faint, sparing of energy.
Yet, like an exiled Government,
With so much jealousy

As were the issue a campaign or Crown,
They hold debates, wage Cabinet intrigues,
Move token forces up and down,
Turn inches into leagues.

Long I was caught up in their twilit strife.
Almost they got me, almost had me weaned
From all my memory of life.
But laughter supervened:

Laughter, like sunlight in the cucumber,
The innermost resource, that does not fail.
I, Marco Polo, traveller,
Am back, with what a tale!

THOMAS CAMPION

'Never weather-beaten Saile more willing bent to shore'

Never weather-beaten Saile more willing bent to shore,
Never tyred Pilgrims limbs affected slumber more,
Then my weary spright now longs to flye out of my troubled brest.
  O come quickly, sweetest Lord, and take my soule to rest.

Ever-blooming are the joyes of Heav'ns high paradice,
Cold age deafes not there our eares, nor vapour dims our eyes;
Glory there the Sun outshines, whose beames the blessed onely see:
  O come quickly, glorious Lord, and raise my spright to thee.

THOMAS CAREW

Persuasions to Love

Think not, 'cause men flatt'ring say
Y' are as fresh as April, sweet as May,
Bright as is the morning star,
That you are so; or, though you are,
Be not therefore proud, and deem
All men unworthy your esteem:
For, being so, you lose the pleasure
Of being fair, since that rich treasure
Of rare beauty and sweet feature
Was bestow'd on you by Nature
To be enjoy'd, and 'twere a sin
There to be scant, where she hath bin
So prodigal of her best graces:

Thus common beauties and mean faces
Shall have more pastime, and enjoy
The sport you lose by being coy.
Did the thing for which I sue
Only concern myself, not you;
Were men so fram'd as they alone
Reap'd all the pleasure, women none;
Then had you reason to be scant:
But 'twere a madness not to grant
That which affords (if you consent)
To you, the giver, more content
Than me, the beggar. Oh, then be
Kind to yourself, if not to me.
Starve not yourself, because you may
Thereby make me pine away;
Nor let brittle beauty make
You your wiser thoughts forsake;
For that lovely face will fail:
Beauty's sweet, but beauty's frail;
'Tis sooner past, 'tis sooner done,
Than summer's rain, or winter's sun;
Most fleeting, when it is most dear,
'Tis gone, while we but say 'tis here.
These curious locks, so aptly twin'd,
Whose every hair a soul doth bind,
Will change their auburn hue, and grow
White and cold as winter's snow.
That eye, which now is Cupid's nest,
Will prove his grave, and all the rest
Will follow; in the cheek, chin, nose,
Nor lily shall be found, nor rose.
And what will then become of all
Those whom now you servants call?
Like swallows, when your summer's done,
They'll fly, and seek some warmer sun.
Then wisely choose one to your friend
Whose love may, when your beauties end,
Remain still firm: be provident,
And think, before the summer's spent,
Of following winter; like the ant,
In plenty hoard for time of scant.
Cull out, amongst the multitude

Of lovers that seek to intrude
Into your favour, one that may
Love for an age, not for a day;
One that will quench your youthful fires,
And feed in age your hot desires.
For when the storms of time have mov'd
Waves on that cheek which was belov'd,
When a fair lady's face is pin'd,
And yellow spread where red once shin'd;
When beauty, youth, and all sweets leave her,
Love may return, but lover never:
And old folks say there are no pains
Like itch of love in aged veins.
O love me, then, and now begin it,
Let us not lose this present minute;
For time and age will work that wrack
Which time or age shall ne'er call back.
The snake each year fresh skin resumes,
And eagles change their aged plumes;
The faded rose each spring receives
A fresh red tincture on her leaves:
But if your beauties once decay,
You never know a second May.
O then, be wise, and whilst your season
Affords you days for sport, do reason;
Spend not in vain your life's short hour,
But crop in time your beauty's flower,
Which will away, and doth together
Both bud and fade, both blow and wither.

CATULLUS

'Lesbia'

Lesbia
       live with me
& love me so
we'll laugh at all
the sour-faced strict-
ures of the wise.
This sun once set
will rise again,
when our sun sets
follows night &
an endless sleep.
Kiss me now a
thousand times &
now a hundred
more & then a
hundred & a
thousand more again
till with so many
hundred thousand
kisses you & I
shall both lose count
nor any can
from envy of
so much of kissing
put his finger
on the number
of sweet kisses
you of me &
I of you,
darling, have had.

Translated by Peter Whigham

'Walpole! I thought not I should ever see'

WALPOLE! I thought not I should ever see
So mean a Heart as thine has proved to be;
Thou, who in Luxury nurs'd behold'st with Scorn
The Boy, who Friendless, Penniless, Forlorn,
Asks thy high Favour, – thou mayst call me Cheat –
Say, didst thou ne'er indulge in such Deceit?

Who wrote Otranto? But I will not chide,
Scorn I will repay with Scorn, and Pride with Pride.
Still, Walpole, still, thy Prosy Chapters write,
And twaddling Letters to some Fair indite,
Laud all above thee, – Fawn and Cringe to those
Who, for thy Fame, were better Friends than Foes
Still spurn the incautious Fool who dares – –

Had I the Gifts of Wealth and Lux'ry shar'd
Not poor and Mean – Walpole! thou hadst not dared
Thus to insult, But I shall live and Stand
By Rowley's side – when Thou art dead and damned

1769

*Intended to have sent the above to Mr. Walpole but my Sister
perswaded me out of it.* T.C.

JOHN CLARE

The Gipsy Camp

The snow falls deep; the Forest lies alone:
The boy goes hasty for his load of brakes,
Then thinks upon the fire and hurries back;
The Gipsy knocks his hands and tucks them up,
And seeks his squalid camp, half hid in snow,
Beneath the oak, which breaks away the wind,
And bushes close, with snow like hovel warm:
There stinking mutton roasts upon the coals,
And the half-roasted dog squats close and rubs,
Then feels the heat too strong and goes aloof;
He watches well, but none a bit can spare,
And vainly waits the morsel thrown away:
'Tis thus they live – a picture to the place;
A quiet, pilfering, unprotected race.

HARTLEY COLERIDGE

Song

The earliest wish I ever knew
Was woman's kind regard to win;
I felt it long ere passion grew,
Ere such a wish could be a sin.

And still it lasts; – the yearning ache
No cure has found, no comfort known:
If she did love, 'twas for my sake,
She could not love me for her own.

The Innocent Ill

Though all thy gestures and discourses be
    Coyn'd and stamp't by *Modestie*,
    Though from thy *Tongue* ne're slipt away
One word which *Nuns* at th' *Altar* might not say,
    Yet such a sweetness, such a grace
    In all thy *speech* appear,
    That what to th' *Eye* a beauteous *face*,
    That thy *Tongue* is to th' *Ear*.
  So cunningly it wounds the heart,
  It strikes such heat through every part,
That thou a *Tempter* worse than *Satan* art.

Though in thy thoughts scarce any Tracks have bin
    So much as of *Original* Sin,
    Such charms thy *Beauty* wears as might
Desires in dying confest *Saints* excite.
    Thou with strange *Adulterie*
    Dost in each breast a *Brothel keep*;
    Awake all men do *lust* for thee,
    And some *enjoy* Thee when they *sleep*.
  Ne're before did *Woman* live,
  Who to such *Multitudes* did give
The *Root* and *cause* of *Sin*, but only *Eve*.

Though in thy breast so quick a *Pity* be,
    That a *Flies Death's* a *wound* to thee.
    Though savage, and rock-hearted those
Appear, that weep not ev'en *Romances* woes.
    Yet ne're before was *Tyrant* known,
    Whose rage was of so large extent,
    The ills thou dost are *whole* thine own,
    Thou'rt *Principal* and *Instrument*,
  In all the deaths that come from you,
  You do the *treble Office* do
Of *Judge*, of *Tort'urer*, and of *Weapon* too.

Thou *lovely Instrument* of *angry Fate,*
　　Which *God* did for our faults create!
　　Thou *Pleasant, Universal Ill,*
Which *sweet* as *Health,* yet like a *Plague* dost *kill!*
　　Thou kind, well-natur'ed *Tyrannie!*
　　Thou *chaste* committer of a *Rape!*
　　Thou *voluntary Destinie,*
　　Which no man *Can,* or *Would* escape!
　So gentle, and so glad to spare,
　So wondrous good, and wondrous fair,
(We know) e'ven the *Destroying Angels* are.

HART CRANE

Episode of Hands

The unexpected interest made him flush.
Suddenly he seemed to forget the pain, –
Consented, – and held out
One finger from the others.

The gash was bleeding, and a shaft of sun
That glittered in and out among the wheels,
Fell lightly, warmly, down into the wound.

And as the fingers of the factory owner's son,
That knew a grip for books and tennis
As well as one for iron and leather, –
As his taut, spare fingers wound the gauze
Around the thick bed of the wound,
His own hands seemed to him
Like wings of butterflies
Flickering in sunlight over summer fields.

The knots and notches, – many in the wide
Deep hand that lay in his, – seemed beautiful.
They were like the marks of wild ponies' play, –
Bunches of new green breaking a hard turf.

And factory sounds and factory thoughts
Were banished from him by that larger, quieter hand
That lay in his with the sun upon it.
And as the bandage knot was tightened
The two men smiled into each other's eyes.

Repose of Rivers

The willows carried a slow sound,
A sarabande the wind mowed on the mead.
I could never remember
That seething, steady leveling of the marshes
Till age had brought me to the sea.

Flags, weeds. And remembrance of steep alcoves
Where cypresses shared the noon's
Tyranny; they drew me into hades almost.
And mammoth turtles climbing sulphur dreams
Yielded, while sun-silt rippled them
Asunder...

How much I would have bartered! the black gorge
And all the singular nestings in the hills
Where beavers learn stitch and tooth.
The pond I entered once and quickly fled –
I remember now its singing willow rim.

And finally, in that memory all things nurse;
After the city that I finally passed
With scalding unguents spread and smoking darts
The monsoon cut across the delta
At gulf gates... There, beyond the dykes

I heard wind flaking sapphire, like this summer,
And willows could not hold more steady sound.

Eternity

September – remember!
October – all over.

Barbadian adage

After it was over, though still gusting balefully,
The old woman and I foraged some drier clothes
And left the house, or what was left of it;
Parts of the roof reached Yucatan, I suppose.
She almost – even then – got blown across lots
At the base of the mountain. But the town, the town!

Wires in the streets and Chinamen up and down
With arms in slings, plaster strewn dense with tiles,
And Cuban doctors, troopers, trucks, loose hens...
The only building not sagging on its knees,
Fernandez' Hotel, was requisitioned into pens
For cotted negroes, bandaged to be taken
To Havana on the first boat through. They groaned.

But was there a boat? By the wharf's old site you saw
Two decks unsandwiched, split sixty feet apart
And a funnel high and dry up near the park
Where a frantic peacock rummaged amid heaped cans.
No one seemed to be able to get a spark
From the world outside, but some rumor blew
That Havana, not to mention poor Batabanó,
Was halfway under water with fires
For some hours since – all wireless down
Of course, there too.

                    Back at the erstwhile house
We shoveled and sweated; watched the ogre sun
Blister the mountain, stripped now, bare of palm,

Everything – and lick the grass, as black as patent
Leather, which the rimed white wind had glazed.
Everything gone – or strewn in riddled grace –
Long tropic roots high in the air, like lace.
And somebody's mule steamed, swaying right by the pump,
Good God! as though his sinking carcass there
Were death predestined! You held your nose already
Along the roads, begging for buzzards, vultures…
The mule stumbled, staggered. I somehow couldn't budge
To lift a stick for pity of his stupor.

                        For I
Remember still that strange gratuity of horses
– One ours, and one, a stranger, creeping up with dawn
Out of the bamboo brake through howling, sheeted light
When the storm was dying. And Sarah saw them, too –
Sobbed, Yes, now – it's almost over. For they know;
The weather's in their noses. There's Don – but that one, white
– I can't account for him! And true, he stood
Like a vast phantom maned by all that memoried night
Of screaming rain – Eternity!

                        Yet water, water!
I beat the dazed mule toward the road. He got that far
And fell dead or dying, but it didn't so much matter.

The morrow's dawn was dense with carrion hazes
Sliding everywhere. Bodies were rushed into graves
Without ceremony, while hammers pattered in town.
The roads were being cleared, injured brought in
And treated, it seemed. In due time
The President sent down a battleship that baked
Something like two thousand loaves on the way.
Doctors shot ahead from the deck in planes.
The fever was checked. I stood a long time in Mack's talking
New York with the gobs, Guantanamo, Norfolk, –
Drinking Bacardi and talking USA.

ELIZABETH DARYUSH

'Autumn, dark wanderer halted here once more'

Autumn, dark wanderer halted here once more,
Grave roamer camped again in our light wood,
With garments ragg'd, but rich and gorgeous-hued,
With the same fraying splendours as before –
Autumn, wan soothsayer, worn gipsy wise,
With melancholy look, but bearing bold,
With lean hard limbs careless of warmth or cold,
With dusky face, and gloomed defiant eyes,

You glanced at summer, and she hung her head;
You gazed, and her fresh cheek with fever burned;
You sighed, and from her flowery vales she turned;
You whispered, and from her fond home she fled:

Now seated by your tattered tent she broods
On timeless heights, eternal solitudes.

'Anger lay by me all night long'

Anger lay by me all night long,
    His breath was hot upon my brow,
He told me of my burning wrong,
    All night he talked and would not go.

He stood by me all through the day,
    Struck from my hand the book, the pen;
He said: 'Hear first what *I've* to say,
    And sing, if you've the heart to, *then.*'

A FIELD OF LARGE DESIRES   45

And can I cast him from my couch?
    And can I lock him from my room?
Ah no, his honest words are such
    That he's my true-lord, and my doom.

Still-Life

Through the open French window the warm sun
lights up the polished breakfast-table, laid
round a bowl of crimson roses, for one —
a service of Worcester porcelain, arrayed
near it a melon, peaches, figs, small hot
rolls in a napkin, fairy rack of toast,
butter in ice, high silver coffee-pot,
and, heaped on a salver, the morning's post.

She comes over the lawn, the young heiress,
from her early walk in her garden-wood
feeling that life's a table set to bless
her delicate desires with all that's good,

that even the unopened future lies
like a love-letter, full of sweet surprise.

from *Orchestra*

'Thus they who first did found a commonweal'

'Thus they who first did found a commonweal,
And they who first religion did ordain,
By dancing first the people's hearts did steal;
Of whom we now a thousand tales do feign.
Yet do we now their perfect rules retain,
And use them still in such devices new
As in the world, long since their withering, grew.

'For after towns and kingdoms founded were,
Between great states arose well-ordered war,
Wherein most perfect measure doth appear;
Whether their well-set ranks respected are
In quadrant forms or semicircular,
Or else the march, when all the troops advance
And to the drum in gallant order dance.

'And after wars, when white-wing'd victory
Is with a glorious triumph beautified,
And every one doth *Io, Io!* cry,
While all in gold the conqueror doth ride,
The solemn pomp that fills the city wide
Observes such rank and measure everywhere
As if they all together dancing were.

'The like just order mourners do observe,
But with unlike affection and attire,
When some great man that nobly did deserve,
And whom his friends impatiently desire,
Is brought with honour to his latest fire.
The dead corpse too in that sad dance is moved,
As if both dead and living dancing loved.

'A diverse cause, but like solemnity,
Unto the temple leads the bashful bride,
Which blusheth like the Indian ivory
Which is with dip of Tyrian purple dyed;
A golden troop doth pass on every side
Of flourishing young men and virgins gay,
Which keep fair measure all the flowery way.

'And not alone the general multitude,
But those choice Nestors, which in council grave
Of cities and of kingdoms do conclude,
Most comely order in their sessions have;
Wherefore the wise Thessalians ever gave
The name of leader of their country's dance
To him that had their country's governance.

'And those great masters of the liberal arts
In all their several schools do dancing teach;
For humble grammar first doth set the parts
Of congruent and well-according speech,
Which rhetoric, whose state the clouds doth reach,
And heavenly poetry do forward lead,
And divers measures diversely do tread.

'For Rhetoric, clothing speech in rich array,
In looser numbers teacheth her to range
With twenty tropes, and turnings every way,
And various figures, and licentious change;
But poetry, with rule and order strange,
So curiously doth move each single pace,
As all is marred if she one foot misplace.

'These arts of speech the guides and marshals are,
But logic leadeth reason in a dance,
Reason, the cynosure and bright lodestar
In this world's sea, to avoid the rocks of chance;
For with close following and continuance
One reason doth another so ensue
As, in conclusion, still the dance is true.

'So music to her own sweet tunes doth trip,
With tricks of 3, 5, 8, 15, and more;

So doth the art of numbering seem to skip
From even to odd, in her proportioned score;
So do those skills, whose quick eyes do explore
The just dimension both of earth and heaven,
In all their rules observe a measure even.

'Lo! this is Dancing's true nobility,
Dancing, the child of Music and of Love;
Dancing itself, both love and harmony,
Where all agree and all in order move;
Dancing, the art that all arts do approve;
The fair character of the world's consent,
The heaven's true figure, and the earth's ornament.'

GAIL DENDY

The Coin of Africa

It's the different images

stretched rib-raw across i-Afrika,
i-worn-shod tale of
one-man-one-eye an' i-tooth for jaw.
We a-jump; tune's fine, hoki.
No-like – no problem, a-eeezy
AK-47 dum-dum, rut-tut-tut-tut!

And sometimes they throw the bones and strip
that cock's feathers bloody while the goat
long ago left its guts on the beach.
They're smeared in thick yellow
ochre, crusty and fly-stained, old
in the melting-pot, a sizzling pong
of ulnas and femurs and baby's ears
panga-ed with fury and incantations.

Assault

Oh Daddy
he held me
strong between his hands
and turned me
upside down
I laughed
giddy and happy

he held me
his hand on my head
and my heart
bang-bang whistle
never stopped
loving him

I sat
tugging at him
while I played
jumping up and down
merrily
the air in tune
tinkel like tinseltown

he turned me
upside down
and in a flash
I remembered
this man wasn't
my father.

Goodbye and All That

Goodbye and all that,
rushing helter skelter

The willows bend
their heads
'shake-me-slowly', groans
the finch, untutored
in the science
of vindication.

I phoned – where were you
among the wire strands,
the frayed fabric
echoing nowhere.
Where were you
when you answered?

(Chill winds blue
and dry as your eye
saying your 'hello'
meant only 'goodbye'.)

You knew strewn
syllables, thorn-sharp,
would prick blood
from my heart.
You knew it to be so.
You knew, you knew.

Break the barrier,
throw back the mattress,
cut and close
this episode.

I gave you up
for Lent; yes,
I rounded you
into a sticky bun
and ate you
like a sacrament.

EMILY DICKINSON

'To lose one's faith – surpass'

To lose one's faith – surpass
The loss of an Estate –
Because Estates can be
Replenished – faith cannot –

Inherited with Life –
Belief – but once – can be –
Annihilate a single clause –
And Being's – Beggary –

ERNEST DOWSON

Vitae Summa Brevis Spem Nos Vetat Incohare Longam

They are not long, the weeping and the laughter,
    Love and desire and hate:
I think they have no portion in us after
        We pass the gate.

They are not long, the days of wine and roses:
    Out of a misty dream
Our path emerges for a while, then closes
        Within a dream.

'*I would have chosen children*'

I would have chosen children,
the breathing hearth. And made my own
ritual in winter, birth and bone.
Not this wordy ferment in the fingers,
this sailing hunger capsized in the breast.
I would have chosen children,
and roofed with rose of fire their early east.

1946

'*He for whose sake*'

He for whose sake this ambiguity
leads me by wilderness and careless waters
towards my dear resurrection, still maintains
forever my watching breath stilled for his coming.

My harlot self in crimsons
blesses where summer shines
his name upon the stones.

In the blaze of my veins' history
his law-breaking mercury
changes each voice I carry.

All thoughts are passport to his quiet room.
My searching joy without least let or hindrance
brings back imagined news from his last glance.
His breath my life, my death were his indifference.

1947

LAWRENCE DURRELL

Nobody

You and who else?
Who else? Why Nobody.
I shall be weeks or months away now
Where the diving roads divide,
A solitude with little dignity,
Where forests lie, where rivers pine,
In a great hemisphere of loveless sky:
And your letters will cross mine.

Somewhere perhaps in a cobweb of skyscrapers
Between Fifth and Sixth musing I'll go,
Matching some footprints in young snow,
Within the loving ambush of some heart,
So close and yet so very far apart...
I don't know, I just don't know.

Two beings watching the skyscrapers fade,
Rose in the falling sleet or
Phantom green, licking themselves
Like great cats at their toilet,
Licking their paws clean.
I shall hesitate and falter, that much I know.

Moreover, do you suppose, you too
When you reach India at last, as you will,
I'll be back before two empty coffee cups
And your empty chair in our shabby bistro;
You'll have nothing to tell me either, no,
Not the tenth part of a sigh to exchange.

Everything will be just so.
I'll be back alone again
Confined in memory, but nothing to report,
Watching the traffic pass and
Dreaming of footprints in the New York snow.

1971

A Patch of Dust

In all this summer dust O Vincent
You passed through my loyal mind,
And I saw the candlepower of stored light,
Like water in the humps of camels or in
Canopies of fire smouldering in volcanoes
Like ancient prostitutes or doges.
Memory giving the ikon of love a morbid kiss!

It doesn't matter; in the silent night
Fragrant with the death of so many friends, poets,
The major darkness comes and art beckons
With its quiet seething of the writer's mind.

Your great canvas humming like a top.
But the terror for me is that you didn't realise
That love, even in inferior versions, is a kind
Of merciful self-repair. O Vincent you were blind.
Like some great effluent performer
Discharging whole rivers into hungry seas.
I do not mean the other kind of love,
Born in newspapers like always exchanging
Greasy false teeth. Not of that kind.

In these shining canvases I commend
A fatal diagnosis of light, more light;
Famous last words to reach the inessential.
They seem to assume that death is unnecessary
And in discreet images make ethical strife stationary,
Signposting always desires at bay.
Goodness! It is canny in its way.

Because the irritation of light leads onwards
Towards blindness which is truth, an unknowing,
And the constraints of unlucky companionship
Hinder like a foolish marriage. One must act.
It is no good explaining things with unction,
You will never get beyond their primal function.

But you directly saw the splendour of the
Dying light redeemed. Have mercy on us!

You went mad, they say, the companionship
Of angels grew too loud to bear. You felt
That what was done was quite beyond repair.
So madness, why not? An irrational respect
For tin or pincushions, a whole architecture.
The girl you loved was grave yet debonair
Like the French whore I live with I suppose.
And dying of self-importance is the usual thing;
The creed of loneliness is all that's left,
And art, the jack o'lantern to console and punish.
All this I saw in a patch of dust at St Remy
During the fatal year of 1974.

1974

KATE ELLIS

---

festivals of mouthpieces

Something sublime
had eaten its way into the room,
incredulous time
sank the party into the circular mind,

while childhood in its grace
ran circles above you;
you took to a crawl
from noise and rhyme,

to stand
at the pirated form,
something black or white,
a beautiful syndrome of your mind.

Those creatures do remonstrate,
water the remainder,
as they armour age,
bemused at your eager breakfast eyes

staring
into bereaved menus of incredible names.
You let it all go,
you rot the water that told.

---

from *The Name of This Poem Is Always the Same*

'— all that concrete, steel'

       — all that concrete, steel,
and glass. We've seen what it was

to clear the wreckage from 9/11,
   a scant few blocks on the order
of months. It makes the world seem awfully

   big and set in its ways,
but it ain't, it shakes out smaller than we think.
   I am thinking of eggshells too thin

to hatch, skulls and cross-bones, about
   how Mom in the '40's stopped using
DDT. She got the damned stuff,

   at Safeway, y'know. Imagine,
Safeway! Bull! An' us kids would get it
   an' spray it on flies to watch them

drop off the wall, an' then at each other –
   caught by the chiff at the edge
of the smell, the way that airplane dope

   or ethyl at the pump has an edge.
What did we know? or any of us know?
   or what did we any of us think

we knew? I'll mention thalidomide only,
   the calming effects on expectant
mothers, the fetal defects in babies.

   So what's the latest now after
we're dead on drugs that kill the aches
   and pains that come with the years?

JAMES ELROY FLECKER

The Translator and the Children

While I translated Baudelaire,
Children were playing out in the air.
Turning to watch, I saw the light
That made their clothes and faces bright.
I heard the tune they meant to sing
As they kept dancing in a ring;
But I could not forget my book,
And thought of men whose faces shook
When babies passed them with a look.

They are as terrible as death,
Those children in the road beneath.
Their witless chatter is more dread
Than voices in a madman's head:

Their dance more awful and inspired,
Because their feet are never tired,
Than silent revel with soft sound
Of pipes, on consecrated ground,
When all the ghosts go round and round.

Oxford Canal

When you have wearied of the valiant spires of this County Town,
    Of its wide white streets and glistening museums, and black
                                        monastic walls,
    Of its red motors and lumbering trams, and self-sufficient people,
    I will take you walking with me to a place you have not seen –
    Half town and half country – the land of the Canal.
    It is dearer to me than the antique town: I love it more than the
                                        rounded hills:
    Straightest, sublimest of rivers is the long Canal.
    I have observed great storms and trembled: I have wept for fear
                                        of the dark,
    But nothing makes me so afraid as the clear water of this idle
                                        canal on a summer's noon.
    Do you see the great telephone poles down in the water, how
                                        every wire is distinct?
    If a body fell into the canal it would rest entangled in those wires
                                        for ever, between earth and air.
    For the water is as deep as the stars are high.
    One day I was thinking how if a man fell from that lofty pole
    He would rush through the water toward me till his image was
                                        scattered by his splash,
    When suddenly a train rushed by: the brazen dome of the engine
                                        flashed: the long white carriages roared;
    The sun veiled himself for a moment, and the signals loomed in
                                        fog;
    A savage woman screamed at me from a barge: little children
                                        began to cry;
    The untidy landscape rose to life; a sawmill started;
    A cart rattled down to the wharf, and workmen clanged over the
                                        iron footbridge;

A beautiful old man nodded from the first story window of a
                                          square red house,
And a pretty girl came out to hang up clothes in a small delightful
                                          garden.
O strange motion in the suburb of a county town: slow regular
                              movement of the dance of death!
Men and not phantoms are these that move in light.
Forgotten they live, and forgotten die.

B.H. FRASER

Business Centre

1

Business centre. The television is
    on. Somebody has a headache.
Aircraft leaflet the area,
    Margaret Thatcher is on the radio.
A bank manager addresses rotary.
    Someone sets fire to the kitchen.
Sit then perfectly still and be
    kissed.

2

John, or Nanki-Poo
    dedicated to that certainty which
disappeared with miners and
    Handel's requiem in Old Trafalgar
at Christmas.
    Rise then Metroland although
the warmth is that
    of unkept places at Euston.

3

Property values rise steadily
    in the background: foreign investors
at Luton-sur-Mer.
The Greek was dejected that day
    and went the whole hog at auction
in memory of his mother, an
    illegitimate Mitford.

4

Blessings on the Harvest Festival.
    I shall contribute an onion.
Or sponsor the cricket team to
    advertise my undertakings on their
flannels in deo excelsis so
    something is tasteful in
suburbia. Where I Am.

5

Hitler and Stalin are the names
    of the dogs that roam our streets
after dark. Purchased from
    a friend, whose sister has a
brother whose sister is the
    receptionist at the business
centre in England.

GEORGE GASCOIGNE

The Green Knight's Farewell to Fancy

Fancy (quoth he) farewell, whose badge I long did bear,
And in my hat full harebrainedly, thy flowers did I wear:
Too late I find (at last), thy fruits are nothing worth,
Thy blossoms fall and fade full fast, though bravery bring them forth.
By thee I hoped always, in deep delights to dwell,
But since I find thy fickleness, *Fancy* (quoth he) *farewell.*

Thou mad'st me live in love, which wisdom bids me hate,
Thou bleared'st mine eyes and mad'st me think, that faith was mine
                                                        by fate:
By thee those bitter sweets, did please my taste alway,
By thee I thought that love was light, and pain was but a play:
I thought that beauty's blaze, was meet to bear the bell,
And since I find myself deceived, *Fancy* (quoth he) *farewell.*

The gloss of gorgeous courts, by thee did please mine eye,
A stately sight me thought it was, to see the brave go by:
To see their feathers flaunt, to mark their strange device,
To lie along in ladies' laps, to lisp and make it nice:
To fawn and flatter both, I likéd sometime well,
But since I see how vain it is, *Fancy* (quoth he) *farewell.*

When court had cast me off, I toiléd at the plough
My fancy stood in strange conceits, to thrive I wote not how:
By mills, by making malt, by sheep and eke by swine,
By duck and drake, by pig and goose, by calves and keeping kine:
By feeding bullocks fat, when price at markets fell,
But since my swains eat up the gains, *Fancy* (quoth he) *farewell.*

In hunting of the deer, my fancy took delight,
All forests knew, my folly still, the moonshine was my light:
In frosts I felt no cold, a sunburnt hue was best,
I sweat and was in temper still, my watching seeméd rest:
What dangers deep I passed, it folly were to tell,
And since I sigh to think thereon, *Fancy* (quoth he) *farewell.*

A fancy fed me once, to write in verse and rhyme,
To wray my grief, to crave reward, to cover still my crime:
To frame a long discourse, on stirring of a straw,
To rumble rhyme in raff and ruff, yet all not worth a haw:
To hear it said there goeth, the *man that writes so well*,
But since I see, what poets be, *Fancy* (quoth he) *farewell*.

At music's sacred sound, my fancies eft begun,
In concords, discords, notes and clefs, in tunes of unison:
In *Hierarchies* and strains, in rests, in rule and space,
In monochords and moving modes, in *Burdens* underbass:
In descants and in chants, I strainéd many a yell,
But since musicians be so mad, *Fancy* (quoth he) *farewell*.

To plant strange country fruits, to sow such seeds likewise,
To dig and delve for new found roots, where old might well suffice:
To proyne the water boughs, to pick the mossy trees,
(Oh how it pleased my fancy once) to kneel upon my knees,
To griff a pippin stock, when sap begins to swell:
But since the gains scarce quit the cost, *Fancy* (quoth he) *farewell*.

Fancy (quoth he) *farewell*, which made me follow drums,
Where powdered bullets serves for sauce, to every dish that comes,
Where treason lurks in trust, where *Hope* all hearts beguiles,
Where mischief lieth still in wait, when fortune friendly smiles:
Where one day's prison proves, that all such heavens are hell,
And such I feel the fruits thereof, *Fancy* (quoth he) *farewell*.

If reason rule my thoughts, and God vouchsafe me grace,
Then comfort of philosophy, shall make me change my race,
And fond I shall it find, that Fancy sets to show,
For weakly stands that building still, which lacketh grace by low:
But since I must accept, my fortunes as they fell,
I say God send me better speed, and *Fancy now farewell*.

DAVID GASCOYNE

The cold renunciatory beauty

The cold renunciatory beauty of those who would die
to hide their love from scornful fingers of the drab
is not that which glistens like wing or leaf in eyes
of erotic statues standing breast to chest
on high and open mountainside.

Complex draws tighter like a steel wire mesh
about the awkward bodies of those born under shame,
striping the tender flesh with blood like tears
flowing; their love they dare not name;
Each is divided by desire and fear.

The young sons of the hopeless blind shall strike
matches in the marble corridor and find
their bodies cool and white as the stone walls,
and shall embrace, emerging like mingled springs
onto the height to face the fearless sun.

A Tough Generation

To grow unguided at a time when none
Are sure where they should plant their sprig of trust;
When sunshine has no special mission to endow
With gold the rustic rose, which will run wild
And ramble from the garden to the wood
To train itself to climb the trunks of trees
If the old seedsman die and suburbs care
For sentimental cottage-flowers no more;
To grow up in a wood of rotted trees
In which it is not known which tree will be

First to disturb the silent sultry grove
With crack of doom, dead crackling and dread roar –
Will be infallibly to learn that first
One always owes a duty to oneself;
This much at least is certain: one must live.
And one may reach, without having to search
For much more lore than this, a shrewd maturity,
Equipped with adult aptitude to ape
All customary cant and current camouflage;
Nor be a whit too squeamish where the soul's concerned,
But hold out for the best black market price for it
Should need remind one that one has to live.
Yet just as sweetly, where no markets are,
An unkempt rose may for a season still
Trust its own beauty and disclose its heart
Even to the woodland shade, and as in sacrifice
Renounce its ragged petals one by one.

GEOFFREY GODBERT

Of course you are beautiful

Of course you are beautiful:
I can measure it with a broken stick,
except on the day the wind blew
across the beauty I mean, across the fields,
into the hair of the trees, rousing
the surface of ponds and turned you
like an ordinary leaf
of such uncatchable beauty.

GREY GOWRIE

From Primrose Hill

an altercation of tower block
buildings with estuarine
sky. It is the turn
of our century, two hundred years

since William Blake
walked where we are standing,
and two thousand
from his conscript Lamb.

Sheep, certainly,
grazed in Regent's Park
at the last turn, over there
to the left of the Zoo,

and back in your car,
on audio-tape,
Milly Theale watched them
after the great physician

told her 'Live all you can,'
quick as she could. Money
delivered her heart's wish
but did for her friends.

Today you need money
to live hereabouts,
yet the knot of children
grappling with kites

or keening a little
in the February wind,
are constant, hail
from no specially defined

socio-economic
nursery: tracksuits, trainers,
anoraks and baseball
caps worn backward are quids

in the town over.
On foot, on scooters,
or hooded like novitiate
monks they weave in the shade

of a lofted kite
which merrily, merrily
on high blots out
the white winter sun,

the Post Office Tower –
renamed now: one
good building since World War Two –
and, just for a second,

a grey jet swimming lazily
along an upended Thames
like a great shark lunging
its way to Heathrow.

Imagine all the people
John Lennon sang,
X, when we were young.
And we do imagine them

now in the shape of children
sheltered from history
by post-Cold War
arrangement: the kids

born since the Wall came down.
They are the common
life of the city and one –
a grandchild – we hold in common.

He will reach our age
in the twenty fifties.

The way things are going
a gene-tapestry

will unravel for him
at fingertip touch
an archaeology of kin
with all mankind.

May he know where he stands
in the *demos* of DNA –
logged like the veins
and conduits of this place,

the ciphers, underground seams
opening now before us – ;
know the random miracle
of being wired to the world.

Prayers like this
stop short in the wind,
in flux like traffic
seeping down the road

that abuts our hill
and dissolves in a delta
of Camden Town.
Nothing, we fear,

will change overmuch –
pray all the same.
The cerebellum
of a twelve year old

is pliable; soon
it may harden and beat
against the wall
of collective ill.

Desire's arrow,
like love or money,
burns for territory.
Not far from here

the Rolex killers
emptied their guns
into a family
for status seeking.

Footpads with mobiles
stalk Mercs and Beemers
to run to the Balkans.
Be clothed, we were taught,

in humility. The spires,
churches which jostle
for breathing space
on the Canaletto sleeve

of an old LP –
Haydn's 104th
blessed by Klemperer –
are obscured by Canary

Wharf and the NatWest
Tower; St Paul's,
almost as secular,
billows between them.

From this eminence,
with half-shut eyes,
we conjure the blurred blue
of pre-Roman London:

vegetative, boar-infested,
tribal as Ireland.
We have been here before,
will revert again.

But now a terrific
tea is in prospect:
the happy, diurnal
douceur de vivre.

We turn down a hill
which has seen it all;

where, in the dark years,
when we came in,

multitudes gathered
to watch London burning;
the virus we caught
ourselves over Dresden –

that ill reward
for the spatchcocked body
and carbon head
of the unknown civilian

who descends still with blazing
mercy for our kind
for Coronation fireworks, Jubilees, the 'new
millennial experience' – oh so

many years now! so many
people to contrive
a civilisation
and keep it alive.

W.S. GRAHAM

Letter VI

A day the wind was hardly
Shaking the youngest frond
Of April I went on
The high moor we know.
I put my childhood out
Into a cocked hat
And you moving the myrtle

Walked slowly over.
A sweet clearness became.
The Clyde sleeved in its firth
Reached and dazzled me.
I moved and caught the sweet
Courtesy of your mouth.
My breath to your breath.
And as you lay fondly
In the crushed smell of the moor
The courageous and just sun
Opened its door.
And there we lay halfway
Your body and my body
On the high moor. Without
A word then we went
Our ways. I heard the moor
Curling its cries far
Across the still loch.

The great verbs of the sea
Come down on us in a roar.
What shall I answer for?

The Beast in the Space

Shut up. Shut up. There's nobody here.
If you think you hear somebody knocking
On the other side of the words, pay
No attention. It will be only
The great creature that thumps its tail
On silence on the other side.
If you do not even hear that
I'll give the beast a quick skelp
And through Art you'll hear it yelp.

The beast that lives on silence takes
Its bite out of either side.
It pads and sniffs between us. Now

It comes and laps my meaning up.
Call it over. Call it across
This curious necessary space.
Get off, you terrible inhabiter
Of silence. I'll not have it. Get
Away to whoever it is will have you.

He's gone and if he's gone to you
That's fair enough. For on this side
Of the words it's late. The heavy moth
Bangs on the pane. The whole house
Is sleeping and I remember
I am not here, only the space
I sent the terrible beast across.
Watch. He bites. Listen gently
To any song he snorts or growls
And give him food. He means neither
Well or ill towards you. Above
All, shut up. Give him your love.

Greenock at Night I Find You

1

As for you loud Greenock long ropeworking
Hide and seeking rivetting town of my child
Hood, I know we think of us often mostly
At night. Have you ever desired me back
Into the set-in bed at the top of the land
In One Hope Street? I am myself lying
Half-asleep hearing the rivetting yards
And smelling the bone-works with no home
Work done for Cartsburn School in the morning.

At night. And here I am descending and
The welding lights in the shipyards flower blue
Under my hopeless eyelids as I lie
Sleeping conditioned to hide from happy.

2

So what did I do? I walked from Hope Street
Down Lyndoch Street between the night's words
To Cartsburn Street and got to the Cartsburn Vaults
With half an hour to go. See, I am back.

3

See, I am back. My father turned and I saw
He had the stick he cut in Sheelhill Glen.
Brigit was there and Hugh and double-breasted
Sam and Malcolm Mooney and Alastair Graham.
They all were there in the Cartsburn Vaults shining
To meet me but I was only remembered.

ROBERT GRAVES

Despite and Still

Have you not read
The words in my head,
And I made part
Of your own heart?
We have been such as draw
The losing straw –
You of your gentleness,
I of my rashness,
Both of despair –
Yet still might share
This happy will:
To love despite and still.
Never let us deny

The thing's necessity,
But, O, refuse
To choose
Where chance may seem to give
Loves in alternative.

1941

What We Did Next

What we did next, neither of us remembers…
Still, the key turned, the wide bronze gate creaked open
And there before us in profuse detail
Spread Paradise: its lawns dappled with petals,
Pomegranate trees in quincunx, corn in stooks;
Plantations loud with birds, pools live with fish,
And unborn children blue as bonfire-smoke
Crouching entranced to see the grand serpent
Writhe in and out of long rock-corridors,
Rattling his coils of gold –
Or the jewelled toad from whose immense mouth
Burst out the four great rivers… To be there
Was always to be there, without grief, always,
Superior to all chance, or change, or death…

What we did next, neither of us remembers.

1969

Ouzo Unclouded

Here is ouzo (she said) to try you:
Better not drowned in water,
Better not chilled with ice,
Not sipped at thoughtfully,
Nor toped in secret.
Drink it down (she said) unclouded
At a blow, this tall glass full,
But keep your eyes on mine
Like a true Arcadian acorn-eater.

1961

FULKE GREVILLE, LORD BROOKE

'Man, dream no more of curious mysteries'

Man, dream no more of curious mysteries,
As what was here before the world was made,
The first man's life, the state of Paradise,
Where Heaven is, or Hell's eternal shade,
    For God's works are like him, all infinite;
    And curious search, but crafty sin's delight.

The flood that did, and dreadful fire that shall,
Drown, and burn up the malice of the earth,
The divers tongues, and Babylon's downfall,
Are nothing to the man's renewed birth;
    First, let the Law plough up thy wicked heart,
    That Christ may come, and all these types depart.

When thou hast swept the house that all is clear,
When thou the dust hast shaken from thy feet,
When God's all-might doth in thy flesh appear,
Then seas with streams above thy sky do meet;
    For goodness only doth God comprehend,
    Knows what was first, and what shall be the end.

ANGELA HALL

She Always Sang

She always sang – she sang around the house
And in her morning bath – she sang in shops
And as she drove the car – but then she married
And within a year the singing stopped.

Her husband, if not kind, was not unkind –
It was not what he said but what he did not
Say – what he did, but what he failed
To do – what he remembered, but forgot –

What – quite simply – he was not. For thirty
Years she lived a life of songless grief
And when he died she did not cry, but in
Her bath she sang once more for sheer relief.

IAN HAMILTON

Almost Nothing

It is an almost-nothing thing, I know
But it won't let me go. It's not a scent
Exactly, but on hot days or at night I do remember it
As slightly burnt, or over-ripe:
Black wheatfields, sulphur, skin.
It's noiseless too
Although from time to time I think I've heard it
Murmuring: a prayer
Presumably, a promise or a plea. And no,
It's not at all substantial; that's to say
It's substanceless, it's not a thing
That you could touch or see.

It doesn't hurt but it belongs to me.
What do we call it then,
This something in the air, this atmosphere,
This imminence?
Today, because you've turned away,
I'll call it nothing much,
I'll call it, since you're frightened, here to stay.

Biography

Who turned the page? When I went out
Last night, his Life was left wide-open,
Half-way through, in lamplight on my desk:
The Middle Years.
Now look at him. Who turned the page?

Rose

In the delicately shrouded heart
Of this white rose, a patient eye,
The eye of love,
Knows who I am, and where I've been
Tonight, and what I wish I'd done.

I have been watching this white rose
For hours, imagining
Each tremor of each petal to be like a breath
That silences and soothes.
'Look at it', I'd say to you
If you were here: 'it is a sign
Of what is brief, and lonely
And in love.'

But you have gone and so I'll call it wise:
A patient breath, an eye, a rose
That opens up too easily, and dies.

JOHN HEATH-STUBBS

Prayer to Saint Lucy

At this our solstice of history,
Santa Lucia, pray for me –
You, whose too bright, offending eyes
Like leonids fell from your face of skies:
Since I must do my difficult work,
Sixty per cent, at least, in the dark,
Ascended virgin make petition
I am not quite blinded by erudition,
Lest the blank pride of intellect

My senses, or my heart, infect.
These are the years where, still in vain,
We scan the unlimited heavens of pain,
Searching for an absconded God
(Yet under judgment, under His rod);
But may your wintry feast disclose
The first snowdrop, the Christmas rose –
Those white-clothed virgins of the earth,
The naked maiden, the plant of birth –
And faith is the substance of things not seen,
Under the snows of time, the green
Shoots of eternity; so, eyes being gone,
Still, still in the heart, the sun shines on.

The Green Man's Last Will and Testament

An Eclogue for Adrian Risdon

In a ragged spinney (scheduled
For prompt development as a bijou housing estate)
I saw the green daemon of England's wood
As he wrote his testament. The grey goose
Had given him one of her quills for a pen;
The robin's breast was a crimson seal;
The long yellow centipede held a candle.

He seemed like a hollow oak-trunk, smothered with ivy:
At his feet or roots clustered the witnesses,
Like hectic toadstools, or pallid as broom-rape:
Wood-elves – goodfellows, hobs and lobs,
Black Anis, the child-devouring hag,
From her cave in the Dane Hills, saucer-eyed
Phantom dogs, Black Shuck and Barghest, with the cruel nymphs
Of the northern streams, Peg Powler of the Tees
And Jenny Greenteeth of the Ribble,
Sisters of Bellisama, the very fair one.

'I am sick, I must die,' he said. 'Poisoned like Lord Randal
From hedges and ditches. My ditches run with pollution,
My hedgerows are gone, and the hedgerow singers.
The rooks, disconsolate, have lost their rookery:
The elms are all dead of the Dutch pox.
No longer the nightjar churns in the twilit glade,
Nor the owl, like a white phantom, silent-feathered
Glides to the barn. The red-beaked chough,
Enclosing Arthur's soul, is seen no more
Wheeling and calling over the Cornish cliffs.
Old Tod has vacated his deep-dug earth;
He has gone to rummage in the city dustbins.
Tiggy is squashed flat on the M1.

My delicate deer are culled, and on offshore islands
My sleek silkies, where puffin and guillemot
Smother and drown in oil and tar.
The mechanical reaper has guillotined
Ortygometra, though she was no traitor,
Crouching over her cradle – no longer resounds
Crek-crek, crek-crek, among the wheatfields,
Where the scarlet cockle is missing and the blue cornflower.
My orchids and wild hyacinths are raped and torn,
My lenten lilies and my fritillaries.
Less frequent now the debate
Of cuckoo and nightingale – and where is the cuckoo's maid,
The snake-necked bird sacred to Venus,
Her mysteries and the amber twirling wheel?
In no brightness of air dance now the butterflies –
Their hairy mallyshags are slaughtered among the nettles.
The innocent bats are evicted from the belfries,
The death-watch remains, and masticates history

'I leave to the people of England
All that remains:
Rags and patches – a few old tales
And bawdy jokes, snatches of song and galumphing dance-steps.
Above all my obstinacy – obstinacy of flintstones
That breed in the soil, and pertinacity
Of unlovely weeds – chickweed and groundsel,
Plantain, shepherd's purse and Jack-by-the-hedge.
Let them keep it as they wander in the inhuman towns.

'And the little children, imprisoned in ogrish towers, enchanted
By a one-eyed troll in front of a joyless fire –
I would have them remember the old games and the old dances:
Sir Roger is dead, Sir Roger is dead,
She raised him up under the apple tree;
Poor Mary is a-weeping, weeping like Ariadne,
Weeping for her husband on a bright summer's day.'

Quatrains

The Dog Star now, negating all desires,
Hurls through the atmosphere destructive fires;
    In mute indifference heart and pen must lie,
Though Fame still tarries, and though Love expires.

For we have seen the rage of Time consume
Those temples which the Muses' lamps illume;
    If their resplendent torches gutter down,
To smoulder on shall burnt-out stubs presume?

Some verses still unpublished I avow…
A sausage-roll, a pint of beer – but Thou?
    The Thou whose image prompts my midnight tears
Is ash at Mortlake Crematorium now.

The leaves made languid under August skies
In Bloomsbury Square reproach my life; and cries
    The voice Verlaine within his prison heard,
And *'Qu'as-tu fait de ta jeunesse?'* it sighs.

Sweet-scented, possibly, the manuscript
Of half my span is closed, and better skipped;
    We slumber in Hope's lap an hour or two
An unquiet sleep – and wake to find we're gypped.

There was a time when the enchanting bird
Of poetry was in my orchards heard –
    The green boughs whitened with ideas in bloom,
And easy on my lips lighted the word.

Fate's discords have unharmonized those tunes,
And blank abstractions blotted out the runes;
   Each finds his loneliness: FitzGerald knew
Like impotence among the Suffolk dunes.

Time with unpitying and iron feet
Bears down upon us all; we learn to greet,
   Without despair, the inevitable void,
Whether in Nishapur or Russell Street.

Little Russell Street, Bloomsbury
August 1953

EDWARD, LORD HERBERT OF CHERBURY

A Description

I sing her worth and praises high,
Of whom a poet cannot lie.
The little world the great shall blaze:
Sea, earth her body; heaven her face;
Her hair sunbeams, whose every part
Lightens, inflames each lover's heart,
That thus you prove the axiom true,
Whilst the sun help'd nature in you.
   Her front the white and azure sky,
In light and glory raised high;
Being o'ercast by a cloudy frown,
All hearts and eyes dejecteth down.
   Her each brow a celestial bow,
Which through this sky her light doth show,
Which doubled, if it strange appear,
The sun's likewise is doubled there.
   Her either cheek a blushing morn,

Which, on the wings of beauty borne,
Doth never set, but only fair
Shineth, exalted in her hair.
   Within her mouth, heaven's heav'n, reside
Her words: the soul's there glorifi'd.
   Her nose th' equator of this globe,
Where nakedness, beauty's best robe,
Presents a form all hearts to win.
   Last Nature made that dainty chin,
Which, that it might in every fashion
Answer the rest, a constellation,
Like to a desk, she there did place
To write the wonders of her face.
   In this celestial frontispiece,
Where happiness eternal lies,
First arranged stand three senses,
This heaven's intelligences,
Whose several motions, sweet combin'd,
Come from the first mover, her mind.
   The weight of this harmonic sphere
The Atlas of her neck doth bear,
Whose favours day to us imparts,
When frowns make night in lovers' hearts.
   Two foaming billows are her breasts,
That carry rais'd upon their crests
The Tyrian fish: more white's their foam
Than that whence Venus once did come.
   Here take her by the hand, my Muse,
With that sweet foe to make my truce,
To compact manna best compar'd,
Whose dewy inside's not full hard.
   Her waist's an invers'd pyramis,
Upon whose cone love's trophy is.
   Her belly is that magazine
At whose peep Nature did resign
That precious mould by which alone
There can be framed such a one.
   At th' entrance of which hidden treasure,
Happy making above measure,
Two alabaster pillars stand,
To warn all passage from that land;
At foot whereof engraved is

The sad *Non ultra* of man's bliss.
    The back of this most precious frame
Holds up in majesty the same,
Where, to make music to all hearts,
Love bound the descant of her parts.
    Though all this Beauty's temple be,
There's known within no deity
Save virtues shrin'd within her will.
As I began, so say I still,
I sing her worth and praises high,
Of whom a poet cannot lie.

GEORGE HERBERT

Sin

Lord, with what care hast thou begirt us round!
    Parents first season us: then schoolmasters
    Deliver us to laws; they send us bound
To rules of reason, holy messengers,
Pulpits and sundays, sorrow dogging sin,
    Afflictions sorted, anguish of all sizes,
    Fine nets and stratagems to catch us in,
Bibles laid open, millions of surprises,
Blessings beforehand, ties of gratefulness,
    The sound of glory ringing in our ears.
    Without, our shame; within, our consciences;
Angels and grace, eternal hopes and fears.
    Yet all these fences and their whole array
    One cunning bosom-sin blows quite away.

The Vine

I dream'd this mortal part of mine
Was Metamorphoz'd to a Vine;
Which crawling one and every way,
Enthrall'd my dainty *Lucia.*
Me thought, her long small legs & thighs
I with my *Tendrils* did surprize;
Her Belly, Buttocks, and her Waste
By my soft *Nerv'lits* were embrac'd:
About her head I writhing hung,
And with rich clusters (hid among
The leaves) her temples I behung:
So that my *Lucia* seem'd to me
Young *Bacchus* ravisht by his tree.
My curles about her neck did craule,
And armes and hands they did enthrall:
So that she could not freely stir,
(All parts there made one prisoner.)
But when I crept with leaves to hide
Those parts, which maids keep unespy'd,
Such fleeting pleasures there I took,
That with the fancie I awook;
And found (Ah me!) this flesh of mine
More like a *Stock,* than like a *Vine.*

NAZIM HIKMET

Advice for Someone Going into Prison

If instead of getting the rope
you're thrown inside
for not cutting off hope
from your world, your country, your people;
if you do a ten or fifteen year stretch,
aside from the time you have left
don't say:
'Better to have swung at the end of a rope like a flag.'

You must insist on living.
There may not be happiness
but it is your binding duty
to resist the enemy,
and live one extra day.

Inside, one part of you may live completely alone
like a stone at the bottom of a well.
But the other part of you
must so involve yourself
in the whirl of the world,
that you will shudder on the inside
when outside a leaf trembles on the ground forty days away.

Waiting for a letter inside,
singing melancholic songs,
staying awake all night, eyes glued on the ceiling,
is sweet but dangerous.

Look at your face from shave to shave,
forget how old you are,
protect yourself from lice, and from spring evenings,
and eat your bread to the very last crumb
and don't ever forget the freedom of laughter.

Who knows,
if the woman you love no longer loves you,
it's no small thing,
it's like snapping a green twig
to the man inside.
Inside it's bad to think of roses and gardens.
It's good to think of mountains and seas.

Read and write as much as humanly possible,
and I recommend you do weaving
and silver mirrors.

What I'm saying is that inside, ten years, or fifteen years
or even more can be got through,
they really can:
enough that you never let the precious stone
under your left breast grow dull.

1949

Translated by Richard McKane

The Story of Arachne

Far in the night the stars shimmer;
  Athene the grey-eyed goddess treads
stairs of stars to a soaring palace
  of golden thrones and silken beds.

Down in the day the children hurry
  here along the lane to Arachne's door –
'She's weaving something special today!'
  They sit quite still round the cottage floor.

Arachne's hands like a dance begin
  drawing her pictures from the bright wool.
'How do you do it? Did the goddess Athene
  teach you herself? It's so beautiful!'

'Teach *me*?' The dance of wool stops dead.
  Her voice falls on them like a stone:
'The goddess Athene I never saw!
  My hands learned weaving on their own!'

'Arachne! Sh – don't talk like that,
  she'd be so angry if she heard you,
you know what happens to people who think
  they're as good as the gods – she'd murder you!'

'Let her hear! Goddess of spinning and weaving –
  but who's ever seen her weave or spin?
Let her come to this house for a weaving match!
  She can do what she likes – if I don't win.'

The words are out. But nothing changes,
  no striding footstep, no voice in the air.
And the day goes by, that day, another.
  But no one forgets Arachne's dare.

How long's she been standing there in the doorway,
  that strange old woman, shaking her head?
'Arachne, my girl,' says she, 'you'd better
  ask pardon of the goddess for what you said.'

'Ask pardon? Old woman, you mind your own business!
  It's her I'm expecting – why doesn't she come?'
In a blaze of gold old age has vanished.
  The stranger's answer strikes her dumb:

'She has come. She is here. I am Athene!
  Ask pardon now, but you'll ask too late.
You dare compete with me – you shall:
  go get your shuttle, and weave your fate!'

No more is said, no rules need making.
  Side by side in the cluttered room
goddess and girl are blind to all
  but the stretching of thread on a wooden loom.

Then the hours run – like light on water
  their fingers flicker while rainbows play
round growing tapestries, wools, walls, weavers –
  but who'd dare sit there to watch today?

For grimly and coldly they weave the old stories
  of people punished – or people tricked;
the gods disguised, the gods in triumph:
  picture for picture they match their wits

Till the sun sets. That same moment
  their hands drop. The contest's done!
Weaving as exquisite surely must be
  equal? Or – has Arachne won?

For the goddess trembles as fury fills her –
  or, win or lose, the end's the same:
Arachne's gorgeous cloth she seizes
  and her white hands rip it from the frame.

Like a cry of pain the noise of tearing,
    harsh as she rends it, thread to shred:
she spurns the rags, and with her shuttle
    three times she strikes Arachne's head.

She has gathered a herb from the groves of darkness,
    she sprinkles the girl with its bitter juice.
'You will not die, but you'll learn your lesson –
    I'll put your skill to a different use!'

'We warned you Arachne! Why didn't you listen?'
    They cannot help her, they hear her moan,
she is dwindling down – they stare in horror –
    till she lies at their feet, like a little stone.

Are those her fingers that wove so proudly,
    spread like hairs at her speckled sides?
She will make no sound now. Changed for ever
    she scuttles away to a hole and hides.

Nobody saw the goddess go
    who treads the stairs of the starry dome.
They stand in a huddle, baffled and low –
    but night is falling, they must go home.

Nobody sees, high under the vine-leaves,
    a single thread of silver light
where blessed by the moon a spider spins
    a gift for the world, her web, tonight.

To Morfydd

A voice on the winds,
A voice by the waters,
 Wanders and cries:
Oh! what are the winds?
And what are the waters?
 Mine are your eyes!

Western the winds are,
And western the waters,
 Where the light lies:
Oh! what are the winds?
And what are the waters?
 Mine are your eyes!

Cold, cold, grow the winds,
And wild grow the waters,
 Where the sun dies:
Oh! what are the winds?
And what are the waters?
 Mine are your eyes!

And down the night winds,
And down the night waters,
 The music flies:
Oh! what are the winds?
And what are the waters?
Cold be the winds,
And wild be the waters,
 So mine be your eyes!

1891

The Dark Angel

Dark Angel, with thine aching lust
To rid the world of penitence:
Malicious Angel, who still dost
My soul such subtile violence!

Because of thee, no thought, no thing,
Abides for me undesecrate:
Dark Angel, ever on the wing,
Who never reachest me too late!

When music sounds, then changest thou
Its silvery to a sultry fire:
Nor will thine envious heart allow
Delight untortured by desire.

Through thee, the gracious Muses turn
To Furies, O mine Enemy!
And all the things of beauty burn
With flames of evil ecstasy.

Because of thee, the land of dreams
Becomes a gathering place of fears:
Until tormented slumber seems
One vehemence of useless tears.

When sunlight glows upon the flowers,
Or ripples down the dancing sea:
Thou, with thy troop of passionate powers,
Beleaguerest, bewilderest, me.

Within the breath of autumn woods,
Within the winter silences:
Thy venomous spirit stirs and broods,
O Master of impieties!

The ardour of red flame is thine,
And thine the steely soul of ice:
Thou poisonest the fair design
Of nature, with unfair device.

Apples of ashes, golden bright;
Waters of bitterness, how sweet!
O banquet of a foul delight,
Prepared by thee, dark Paraclete!

Thou art the whisper in the gloom,
The hinting tone, the haunting laugh:
Thou art the adorner of my tomb,
The minstrel of mine epitaph.

I fight thee, in the Holy Name!
Yet, what thou dost, is what God saith:
Tempter! should I escape thy flame,
Thou wilt have helped my soul from Death:

The second Death, that never dies,
That cannot die, when time is dead:
Live Death, wherein the lost soul cries,
Eternally uncomforted.

Dark Angel, with thine aching lust!
Of two defeats, of two despairs:
Less dread, a change to drifting dust,
Than thine eternity of cares.

Do what thou wilt, thou shalt not so,
Dark Angel! triumph over me:
Lonely, unto the Lone I go;
Divine, to the Divinity.

1893

Kissing the Bartender

The summer we kissed across the bar,
I felt sixteen at thirty-six:
as if you were a movie star

I had a crush on from afar.
My chest was flat, my legs were sticks
the summer we kissed across the bar.

Balancing on the rail was hard.
Spilled beer made my elbows stick.
You could have been a movie star,

backlit, golden, lofting a jar
of juice or Bloody Mary mix
the summer we kissed across the bar.

Over the sink, the limes, as far
as you could lean, you leaned. I kissed
the movie screen, a movie star.

Drinks stayed empty. Ashtrays tarred.
The customers got mighty pissed
the summer we kissed across the bar.
Summer went by like a shooting star.

JUDITH KAZANTZIS

The Dump

for Harold Pinter

Where on this bright morning the grandmother rakes for
the leavings of the banquet last night. There was a
feast given in honour of the Ambassador: fish, quail, chickens
suckling pigs, veal and several tints of years of wines. From
California flew on ice plump and well manured strawberries.
From Washington the Ambassador. A charming display to end:
of the traditional costumes of our adored country.
And the well mannered Ambassador is instructed and charmed and
expresses this to our new President, to which the General
lights his cigar.
And today the grandmother rakes back the chicken leg
that the Ambassador forgot to finish as he watched with
crinkling eyes the costume of her tribe. She plucks it
hungrily out of the sweet rot under the sweet
blue sky. Dipped in cigar ash, casseroled in filth, the
chicken bit comes into her skin and bones hand. Dry-eyed,
her stare turns on the city.

MARIUS KOCIEJOWSKI

The Water Clock

for J.

I will construct for you
Out of the words I think
Will work best this clock

Whose running depends upon
A steady flow we shall call
The imagination at work.

You need not be alarmed.
You will not be consumed
In a whirlpool of speech.

This clock is scheduled
By the simplest means,
A hole sized just so,

No bigger no smaller
Than that which the ink
Of this pen runs through.

Only what truly matters
Will be given clearance,
And this you may compose

Into whatever shapes
Will bring you nearer
To what you wish reached.

Do not think this comes
Without you pledging faith.
You must be prepared.

A level must be reached
Before the fulcrum slips,
And the hour is chimed

In so clear a pitch
You will think such sounds
Are made in heaven.

There is no beguiling
This level, not even
With mimicry of form.

You may pretend noon
But a shadow spreads
From where you stand.

And besides, be warned,
The horsemen will know
And will stay unmoved.

Babel

So it has come again –
Only the particulars differ.

There is such commotion.
Stones are gathered
Against a wooden door.

The voices are loud, indistinct.

I imagine torchlight,
A man pushing a wheelbarrow.
One could list endlessly,
Only where would that lead?

This tower they have conjured –
An architecture for the times,
Columns of stagnant air,
Emptiness upon emptiness.

Dying Speech of an Old Philosopher

I strove with none, for none was worth my strife:
    Nature I loved, and next to Nature, Art:
I warm'd both hands before the fire of Life;
    It sinks; and I am ready to depart.

La Balue to Louis XI

1480

At last have mercy: let me out at last:
    This iron cage has warped my very bones.
    Have mercy, by the smile thy little ones
First gave thee! Spare me by the hope thou hast

That Christ will save thee. Have not ten years passed?
    Hast thou not made of me a beast that moans,
    Howls on all-fours? Relent: the throne of thrones
Looks down on thine; thy life like mine ebbs fast.

No, no, I'll curse thee blind; I'll curse thee black
    Of the black death; and, hurling hope away,
I'll pray to God to make me of the pack

Which, in the plains of Hell, by night and day
    Shall yell for ever louder on thy track
And rend an ever-renovated prey!

Chastelard to Mary Stuart

1563

Then send me to my death. But wilt thou rid
　　Thy life of me thereby? If in the gloom
　　Of thy adored and silent balmy room
My ghost should glide, where once I panting hid?

At night thou'lt see me; though thou close thy lid
　　As tightly as they soldered down my tomb,
　　And feel a kiss – thou shalt know well of whom –
Scorch thee as living kisses never did.

When thou shalt die, at Heaven's gate I'll sit
　　And watch the stream of silent souls that wend
Through the great arch, till thou approachest it.

Or if thy doom be flame, I shall descend
　　Through all the caverns where the lost souls flit,
To find and clasp thee at their endless end.

GIACOMO LEOPARDI

The Infinite

This lonely hill was always dear to me,
And this hedgerow, that hides so large a part
Of the far sky-line from my view. Sitting and gazing,
I fashion in my mind what lies beyond –
Unearthly silences, and endless space,
And very deepest quiet; then for a while
The heart is not afraid. And when I hear
The wind come blustering among the trees
I set that voice against this infinite silence:
And then I call to mind Eternity,
The ages that are dead, and the living present
And all the noise of it. And thus it is
In that immensity my thought is drowned:
And sweet to me the foundering in that sea.

1819

Translated by John Heath-Stubbs

RICHARD LOVELACE

To Chloris: Love Made in the First Age

In the nativity of time,
Chloris! it was not thought a crime
   In direct Hebrew for to woo.
Now we make love as all on fire,
Ring retrograde our loud desire,
   And court in English backward too.

Thrice happy was that golden age,
When compliment was constru'd rage,
   And fine words in the centre hid;
When cursed No stain'd no maid's bliss,
And all discourse was summ'd in Yes,
   And naught forbade, but to forbid.

Love, then unstinted, love did sip,
And cherries pluck'd fresh from the lip,
   On cheeks and roses free he fed;
Lasses like Autumn plums did drop,
And lads indifferently did crop
   A flower and a maidenhead.

Then unconfined each did tipple
Wine from the bunch, milk from the nipple,
   Paps tractable as udders were:
Then equally the wholesome jellies
Were squeez'd from olive-trees and bellies,
   Nor suits of trespass did they fear.

A fragrant bank of strawberries,
Diaper'd with violets' eyes,
   Was table, tablecloth, and fare;
No palace to the clouds did swell,
Each humble princess then did dwell
   In the piazza of her hair.

Both broken faith and th' cause of it,
All-damning gold, was damn'd to th' Pit;
   Their troth, seal'd with a clasp and kiss,
Lasted until that extreme day
In which they smil'd their souls away,
   And in each other breath'd new bliss.

Because no fault, there was no tear;
No groan did grate the granting ear;
   No false foul breath their del'cat smell:
No serpent kiss poison'd the taste,
Each touch was naturally chaste,
   And their mere sense a miracle.

Naked as their own innocence,
And unembroider'd from offence
   They went, above poor riches, gay;
On softer than the cygnet's down
In beds they tumbled of their own:
   For each within the other lay.

Thus they did live; thus they did love,
Repeating only joys above,
   And angels were, but with clothes on,
Which they would put off cheerfully
To bathe them in the Galaxy,
   Then gird them with the heavenly zone.

Now, Chloris! miserably crave
The offer'd bliss you would not have,
   Which evermore I must deny;
Whilst, ravish'd with these noble dreams,
And crowned with mine own soft beams,
   Enjoying of myself I lie.

Poem of a Day

Rural Meditations

Behold me
 here – the nightingales'
  apprentice, master
of *la gaya scienza*
 formerly:
  I teach
the living tongues
 to a damp and bleak
  sombre and straggling
village that belongs
 half to La Mancha, half
  to Andalusia.
Winter:
 the fireside:
  in the street
a fine rain falls
 alternately as mist or sleet.
  I
a husbandman in fancy
 dream of fields.
  O Lord,
how well thou dost
 and how
  it rains!
on vineyards and on olive-groves
 fields of barley and of beans:
  a still
a small and steady rain.
 How the sowers of the grain
  will bless
like me
 Your bounteousness,
  and those who live

by gathering
        the olive,
                those who hope
for the fortune of a meal
        and have
                all that they own
in the year's deceitful wheel –
        this
                and every year that's gone.
Rain,
        rain on!
                and alternate
as mist or sleet
        and then again
                reverting to a tenuous rain
rain, Lord, rain!
        My chamber keeps
                a wintry light:
the afternoon
        through rain and glass
                sifts its grey illumination –
a medium where thoughts may pass.
        The clock
                neglected in its corner
looms distinct:
        its tick
                forgotten in its repetitions
now beats on
        within my consciousness
                and boring, bored
a uniform metallic heart
        speaks its one and only part:
                tick
tock:
        in villages like these
                does one catch
the pulse of time?
        Truceless
                before the clock
one, rather, fights
        against monotony
                that, in these villages

alights
        to measure
                the passage of their vacancies.
But, clock, is yours
        this time of mine –
                are mine your hours?
(Tick, tick)
        There was a day
                (tick, tick) that passed
and that which I
        most loved
                death made away.
A knell from far
        fades
                into the rain's
minute, untroubled chime
        that rings against the window panes.
                A husbandman in fancy
I
        return to fields.
                Lord,
how they'll bless
        your bounteousness –
                those
who sow the bread.
        Lord,
                is not the rain you bring
law in the ox-ploughed field
        and in
                the palace of the King?
Bounteous water,
        leave
                behind you, life –
you that go
        drop by drop, and
                spring by spring
and river upon river flow,
        that, like this time
                of weariness supply
the sea
        with transitory life,
                with all that seeks nativity

to germinate
        to spring
                and be.
Be
        merciful
                for you become
tomorrow's
        early ear of grain, and
                you restore
tint in the field
        and in the flesh
                and more:
reason
        madness
                bitterness
the grief that wishes for
        and yet remains unsatisfied
                with all belief.
Dark
        is coming down;
                the wire
reddens within the bulb
        gathering to a glow
                with scarce more show
than wax on a lucifer.
        God only knows
                where (under these tomes, reviews
and scribblings) –
        ah, here they are:
                my spectacles.
New books.
        One
                I open
by Unamuno.
        Oh, the chosen
                cherished spirit
of the Spain that shall inherit
        our coming life
                our resurrection!
This
        teacher of a country school,
                unheard of,

he knows no defection,
  Rector of Salamanca!
   Yours –
the philosophy you call
  dilettante and inconstant
   balanced
upon its slender rope –
  nourishes, great
   Don Miguel
his buried hope.
  Water
   of the good spring,
fugitive
  always; always living;
   poetry –
that cordial thing.
  Architectonic?
   (Do you look
for architecture
  in the wind,
   in the soul's structure?)
Rower,
  sailor
   across that sea
which has no shore.
  Henri Bergson:
   Les données
immédiates
  de la conscience.
   Is this
another Gallic artifice?
  This Bergson
   is a sell – agreed,
Maestro Don Miguel?
  He's no Immanuel Kant –
   it's the immortal somersault
his writings want;
  this devilishly clever Jew
   locates
free will
  within his mind's own gates.
   Ah, well –

every wise man has his problem,
        every idiot his theme.
                And yet
it still would seem
        to matter whether
                we, in a short and evil life
shall live
        as either slaves or free.
                But if
(as the poet shows)
        it's seaward all our living flows –
                all will come
to the same thing.
        Oh, these villages!
                reflections
readings
        annotations
                soon will end
in what they are:
        the yawns
                of Solomon.
Is it all
        solitude of solitudes
                vanity of vanities
as saith Ecclesiastes?
        My waterproof,
                umbrella
and sombrero:
        the rain is moderating –
                shall we go?
Night:
        the talk is on
                in the rear room
at the apothecary's
        where they define
                what makes the liberals such swine
and Don José
        scents consolation
                in the return (predicted)
of the conservative administration,
        all spicing it
                from the inexhaustible resources

of a people's wit:
     'The past
         and future
are the same.
     Others
         like us, will blame
the government.
     All changes,
         comes
and goes.' And then,
     for arbitration:
         'No evil lasts a century
to plague a nation.'
     'And the beans
         have come on splendidly –'
'These rains –'
     'The barley –'
         'And they'll flower
by March
     unless the frost –'
         'The labourers
will count the cost
     in sweat –'
         'Torrents –'
'Seas
     would scarcely quench the thirst of olive trees.'
         'In other days –'
'The rain would rain
     at the Lord's will, then
         as now.' 'Until
tomorrow, gentlemen.'
     Tick
         tock
tick-tock: one
     day has gone
         like any other
says the monotone of the clock.
     My table bears
         les données de la conscience
immédiates.
     It's adequate
         this I

that's fundamental
    and at times
        creative and original, that
mingling in mortality
    its freedom and contingency,
      can feel
can see, and yet
     must overleap the confines
       of its narrow keep.

Baeza, 1913

Translated by Charles Tomlinson

JOHN MASEFIELD

from *Reynard the Fox*

'The lurcher dogs soon shot their bolt'

The lurcher dogs soon shot their bolt,
And the fox raced on by the Hazel Holt,
Down the dead grass tilt to the sandstone gash
Of the Pantry Brook at Tineton Ash.
The loitering water, flooded full,
Had yeast on its lip like raddled wool,
It was wrinkled over with Arab script
Of eddies that twisted up and slipt.
The stepping-stones had a rush about them,
So the fox plunged in and swam without them.

Like a rocket shot to a ship ashore
The lean red bolt of his body tore,
Like a ripple of wind running swift on grass;
Like a shadow on wheat when a cloud blows past,
Like a turn at the buoy in a cutter sailing
When the bright green gleam lips white at the railing.
Like the April snake whipping back to sheath,
Like the gannets' hurtle on fish beneath,
Like a kestrel chasing, like a sickle reaping,
Like all things swooping, like all things sweeping,
Like a hound for stay, like a stag for swift,
With his shadow beside like spinning drift.

Past the gibbet-stock all stuck with nails,
Where they hanged in chains what had hung at jails,
Past Ashmundshowe where Ashmund sleeps,
And none but the tumbling peewit weeps,
Past Curlew Calling, the gaunt grey corner
Where the curlew comes as a summer mourner,
Past Blowbury Beacon, shaking his fleece,
Where all winds hurry and none brings peace;
Then down on the mile-long green decline,
Where the turf's like spring and the air's like wine,
Where the sweeping spurs of the downland spill
Into Wan Brook Valley and Wan Dyke Hill.

Abandonment

He went away
With him he took her sight

He went away
Taking with him her taste

He abandoned her
Taking her touch with him

Leaving her lonely
Her voice in a tunnel

He went away
With him he took the day

Only his shadow remains.

ROBERT NYE

Eurynome

Forgive me, Lord, who do not beg your pardon
Because I serve the lady of the garden,
Our mother Eve, who coupled once in Eden
Under the tree of life with father Adam.
She is Eurynome, the moon, my madam,
And there is none as wise or true or fair
In the wide earth, nor in the upper air.

Not Looking

You notice I never look at you when I speak?
Perhaps you have seen in this something crooked –
A fear of meeting your eyes? You would be right
So to think, for my shame of your knowing is such
I'm frightened of your gaze clean through me
Proving my meaning little to you. Yet it is not just this.

I have a way of not looking, as you see,
Which is also part of a way of seeing.
If I do not return the long stare you offer
To search me with, and you might wish I'd learn,
It is because your presence is too sharp,
Your eyes too dear for my eyes, being poor.

I was never exactly frank, you know.
Besides, it's suitable to talk to smoky air
Knowing you near at hand, inhabiting
The corner of my eye, and half my heart.
If I looked straight at you I might say much;
Might even speak of love, which would not do.

from *On the Bone*

'Forget the fine phrases'

Forget the fine phrases
The quicksilver clasp.
When the heart turns
On the spit of withdrawal
Corpuscles weep.
A burst star
On your breakfast plate
Oh no,
No – my non-friend
There is no such thing
As a loving adieu.

Wearing grey then
The spinster's colour
And the shrew's;
Crocheting curses onto
Hessian;
Eyes weak from it
Like the pale blue of the
Plumbago flower.
But still hoping you would come
At the eleventh hour,
Like those blokes in myths
Your tunic undone
And the lanthorns lit.

The tyrants are on the loose
They wear white.
They take voice lessons
Say their prayers
Sleep well
And have sweet dreams.
The tyrants are on the loose again.

New Year's Eve
In some schloss or other
The Nobs prancing about
Liebchen. Liebchen. Liebchen
And Auf Wiedersehen.
Standing on Von Someone's boots
His kisses brusque as saltpetre
Up...Up.... Up.....
We made it to the chandelier.
A glassy surrender.
Afterwards we exchanged
Names and addresses;
He made lasts for shoes
But in a previous life was an
Emperor.

JULIAN ORDE

Conjurors

This crusty July, blackfly
 And other small, moist flies –
  Whiskers so thin
  They are not felt on skin –
Liking a dry July
 Interrupted the performance
 Of the opening of some flowers.

Nasturtiums' circus balance
 Of little heads and great wheels
  Went heeling sideways
  Under the puny flies'
Procession of slow advance –
 Who could be changed to grease
 By a thumb flicked over a leaf.

And as a leaf I picked
    I saw my fingers smeared with the dead
        And I hated this meek
            Giving-up of ghosts by black
Destructive pests, too quick
    To surrender their flash of daylight,
    – As if a cloud had wiped cows from a field

Everything is eating or eaten
    The compost heap drives its mill as
        Seeds in it sprout
        Castaway plants open out
Into the heat of the garden,
    While nasturtiums here big as umbrellas
    Wear a bright display of caterpillars,

Which have eaten between the spokes.
    Brisk as ponies, three abreast
        They scythe their lanes
            Through sweet and pepper greens
That chequered caterpillars make.
    No other leaf they like to taste;
    Nasturtium their nurse and hostess.

Transparent as your eyelid
    Is this tender leaf's skin,
        It holds no reflection
            Yet in the sun's direction
Is seen, in health, glittered
    With the tips of a pin
    That fade at the first bruising.

Green ivory the stalk
    Snapping with rich oils
        That pulse and push
            To a great umbrella bush
And thrust into gravel walk
    Long messengers on bicycles
    Balancing umbrellas at rightangles.

Of such juices are made caterpillars.
    I put seven in a tray
        With a window of glass
        To watch them ripple past,
Scything from the edges
    Of seven round leaves a day
    And growing – until the 28th of July.

Chosen as conjurors and given
    Cells that bloom like water flowers,
        They do not play
        But heartily try
To prove with perfect conjuring
    Dear life, if dear enough, allows
    A blind dive into a hatful of shadows.

They ate no more. A whisper told
    Them: 'Caterpillars, all begin!'
        Through the night
        They dryly ran about
Until one spun a puff of mould
    To fix his end on, then, to plan,
    He spat a thread to fix him upside down.

Doubled back he spat
    And spun thirty threads in one
        Till he lay within a loop
        Tethered over his fourth hoop,
This thread to keep off bird or rat
    Or the wind or houses falling down,
    For he would melt and hope to live again.

Now all the bright ponies are still
    From Highgate to Angmering,
        For three days wait
        Heads bent in a praying shape,
Contracted and stiffened until
    They recede from the surface dizzily, with pain,
    At speed they take leave of their eyes, legs, brain.

Something has so altered in the night,
    Surely the wind changed to make this?
        The racking caterpillar gone
        And a pale nymph lightly borne
Under the old thread. Might
    It be a ghost? The mask on its face
    Has a beak of gold. It is like a little fish!

It is like a waxen fish
    Filled with green leaves
        With a veiny hint
        Of two wings' imprint,
With a waist, with a twitch-
    Ing tail, with a sheaf
    Of yellow dots. It is hooded like a witch.

It has come among us hooded
    And it has no bones!
        It cannot walk
        It wears a long cloak
But is also naked;
    It is the skin round albumen,
    The caul, the bag about the yolk.

It is nothing but a bud
    Too late for the spring,
        It will wither away
        It will never be a flower,
It will shrink without food,
    It is a vegetable swelling,
    A cyst, a nodule that grew one morning.

It is just a bit of dirt,
    It never grew at all,
        The dropping of a hen
        Got in from the garden,
It will smooth itself out
    Like a table, like a floor, the material
    Of houses; it will spread into a wall.

Oh I cannot make it go
        Though I kill it with my eyes.
                It's a castle of glass ·
                It's a door I cannot pass
It's a hill of snow
        It's an aviary wrapping round the skies,
        It's an aquarium; it's a bed for butterflies.

I have been a stalk, a leaf,
        A grub, a fish with beak of gold.
                I fear the dark
                With a double knock
And I hate intruders – that's the truth.
        And here's the truth: I am half dazzled
        By a fancy, violent and old.

Leave a frog and find a dove,
        Find a dish of blackberries
                Where a snake crept,
                Find an owl in a cobweb
Where a hare slept. Improve
        On these – no metamorphosis
        Awful as caterpillar to chrysalis.

Stare till you've insects in your eyes,
        To see will not this trick explain:
                Head in two
                Nymph bursting through,
Legs and face but worn-out clothes,
        Handsome skin rolled to a hairy grain
        By the faceless babe it could not contain.

A hairy grain is all I spy
        Of the caterpillar proud
                In his carpet coat
                Who so lovingly ate
The burning juices of July;
        Who spun his noose and cast his shroud
        And slept on the groundsheet of the dead.

Unborn are the butterflies of the South
  And the caterpillars gone.
      Images of August
      Are carried in these chaste
Cases which have no mouth
  To lap the rivers of the beans
  Tumbling up out of the ground,

Or touch the peas' cool paste.
  Filled with the dying and the growing in the wrath
      Of their commission
      To achieve transfusion,
Then I can break but not awake,
  Nor hurry that congealing drop of breath
  To build myself one butterfly on earth.

As a face at window palely pressed
  Moves, leaving the glass dark,
      So now this bottle
      Darkens, though a full
Rigged ship awaits tomorrow's test
  Of spindle spars and stays. The clock
  Tells fourteen days have passed in the ark.

Fourteen days, and then a crack!
  A skull-grey face with tendril-coiled
      Antennae; wet
      Wings, in folds yet
Of greenish gold with spots of black,
  And a grey fur back, walk like a child
  Unbalancedly into the world.

The involutions of her early wings
  Invite a finger's cruelty
      To know the damp
      Place where she once dwelt,
Or to deface and itself win
  From each cold hollow, guiltily,
  Some of the dews and dustings of her beauty.

She walks like a boat on the beach
    Dragging her drying sails,
        While the last
        Memory of her past
Shakes from her tail: a bead
    Of amber dew, unnoticed as the shell
    That husked and housed her in its brittle walls.

Climber of curtains, long she'll not hang there;
    Taut are her wings and head-dress.
        She will feed on sweet
        Slippets but will never eat.
She will find her answering angel in the air.
    She will lay her eggs upon nasturtiums' crease
    And will not remember the taste of the leaf.

Suddenly she is soundlessly flapping across the broad
    Floor of the air without a trial;
        The sun takes her
        Across to the blue buddleia.
Out of her depths in air she is not afraid.
    When she reaches the tree she finds it full
    Of her own shapes and becomes indistinguishable.

CLERE PARSONS

Suburban Nature Piece

April who dost abet me with shy smiles
If I made bold by amorous fancy touch
Suddenly with my lips thy shining lips which
Are the smooth tulip and chaste crocus bulb
Lady be swift to pardon me this much

This day cannot long delay his choice between
Whether to be spring or remain winter still
– Behold the impetuous sun flings light like scarves
Of petalled lace to dazzle the ocean and
With silver lance our wintry moods to kill

Sweet month thou dost incite me to review
My fearful ship that hath all hopes in hold
O august barque of destiny bear me on
Safely those difficult and deep tides to where
No bird of fire shall steal my apples of gold

Throw open portholes and notice how the in-
Curved water at our wake is making a green
Drain smooth as glass but it must break
As the present breaks vanishing into the past
Pretending there the gayest days have been

Which is exactly not what either I
Or you really believe rather I swear
We begin here and now and shall throw no
Elegant flowers to sobbing yesterdays
We are not yet collected works my dear

Hail early nervous lucent appearing veil
Of tiniest veined leaf weaving a screen
To hide the bare and winter-weary black
Boles of the sentinel dejected trees
Wood ways shall soon be smelling earthy-clean

And here is the generous almond tree whose pink
Victorian skirt primly resists the wind
The ice-cream man who stands by the park gate
Is lifting towards the sun his commonplace
Simian face which is evil and grey-skinned

For with warm days also his trade revives
The children come with fixed and longing eyes
And with saved pennies as often as they can
To savour the small inverted cones of white
Ice cream surely consumed in Paradise

Amiable month unglove thy lovely hand
And with soft fingers conjure from the waste
Barren dry desolate sandstone of the mind
And stagnant pools of stale and weary thought
Rich water-lilies lightly to be embraced

By rainbow-tailed delirious dragonflies
Whose arrowing vivid sudden amazing flight
In summer stings the quiet bowls of shade
Bestirred by thee my thoughts again shall dive
Into remote space like violet rays of light

Listen my dears the skies are going out
Moonlight shall bathe the sleeping nenuphars
Musicians bring forth your violas-da-gamba
And stab my heart with bronze chords now that night
Gently is brushing the alarmed sky with stars.

Unique Days

My many winters blaze
With winter solstices,
The endless repetition
Of unrepeatable days

Massing in memory till
The pattern is complete;
Remembered as the time
When time was standing still.

Each detail is precise:
Winter, towards midwinter,
Wet roads and streaming roofs
And sun that basked on ice;

The lovers in a dream
Longing themselves together;
The starling boxes high
In hot trees, wet with steam;

The clock hands in a daze
Of sleep, stuck to the dial;
The days like centuries,
The kisses like the days.

Bread

With half a century to pile,
    Unwritten, your conclusions,
    By now, if you're not a halfwit,
You should have lost a few illusions,

    Grasped the pleasure of study,
The laws and secrets of success,
The curse of idleness, the heroism
    Needed for happiness;

    That the powerful kingdom of beasts,
The sleepy kingdom of vegetation
    Await their heroes, giants,
Their altars and their revelation;

That first of all the revelations,
    Father of living and dead,
Gift to the generations, growth
    Of the centuries, is bread;

And a harvest field is not just wheat
    But a page to understand,
    Written about yourself
In your remote forefather's hand,

His very word, his own amazing
Initiative among the birth,
    Sorrow and death that circle
    Their set ways round the earth.

Translated by Michael Harari

Tobacconist's

I am nothing.
Never shall be anything.
Cannot will to be anything.
This apart, I have in me all the dreams of the world.

Windows of my room,
Room of one of the millions in the world about whom nobody
knows who he is
(And if they knew who he is, what would they know?),
You give on the mystery of a street constantly trodden by people,
On a street inaccessible to all thoughts,
Real, impossibly real, certain, strangerly certain,
With the mystery of the things under the stones and lives,
With death to put damp in the walls and white hair on men,
With Destiny to drive the car of all down the roadway of nothing.

I, today, am defeated, as though I knew the truth.
I, today, am lucid, as though I were just going to die
And had no longer any connection with things
Except a leave-taking, this house and this side of the street turning into
The line of carriages of a train, and a whistle blown for departure
From inside my head,
And a jolt to my nerves and a creaking of bones at moving off.
I, today, am perplexed, like a man who has thought and found and
forgotten.
I, today, am divided between the loyalty I owe
To the Tobacconist's on the other side of the street, as a thing real
outside,
And to the sensation that all is dream, as a thing real inside.

I have failed altogether.
As I have not achieved any design, perhaps it was all nothing.
The apprenticeship they gave me –
I've dropped from it out of the window at the back of the house.
I went out into the country with grand designs.

But there I met with only grass and trees,
And when there were people they were just like the rest.
I move from the window, sit down in a chair. What shall I think about?

What do I know of what I shall be, I who don't know what I am?
Be whatever I think? But I think so many things!
And there are so many people thinking of being the same thing of
                              which there cannot be all that many!
Genius? At this moment
A hundred thousand brains are busy dreaming of themselves as
                                      geniuses like me,
And history will not mark – who knows? – even one,
And nothing but manure will be left of so many future conquests.
No, I don't believe in me…
All the lunatic asylums have in them patients with many many
                                      certainties!
And I, who have no certainty at all, am I more certain or less certain?

No, not even in me…
In how many garrets, and non-garrets, in the world
Are there not at this hour geniuses-in-their-own-eyes dreaming?
How many high and noble and lucid aspirations –
Yes, really and truly high and noble and lucid –
And who knows whether realizable? –
Will never see the light of the real sun, or reach the ears of people?
The world is for the person who is born to conquer it,
And not for the one who dreams he can conquer it, even if he be right.
I have dreamed more than Napoleon performed.
I have squeezed into a hypothetical breast more lovingkindnesses
                                      than Christ,
I have made philosophies in secret that no Kant wrote.

But I am, and perhaps always shall be, the man of the garret,
Even though I don't live there;
I shall always be the *one who was not born for that*;
I shall always be the one who *had qualities*;
I shall always be the one who waited for them to open
to him the door at the foot of a wall without a door,
And sang the ballad of the Infinite in a hen-coop,
And heard the voice of God in a well with a lid.
Believe in myself? No, and in nothing.
Let Nature pour out over my ardent head
Her sunshine, her rain, the wind that touches my hair,

And the rest that may come if it will, or have to come, or may not.
Heart-diseased slaves of the stars,
We conquer the whole world before getting out of bed;
But we wake up and it is opaque,
We get up and it is alien,
We go out of the house and it is the entire earth
Plus the solar system and the Milky Way and the Indefinite.

(Have some chocolates, little girl;
Have some chocolates!
Look, there's no metaphysics in the world except chocolates.
Look, all the religions teach no more than the confectioner's.
Eat, dirty little girl, eat!
If I could eat chocolates with the same truth as you do!
But I think and, peeling the silver paper with its fronds of tin,
I leave it all lying on the floor, just as I have left life.)

But at least there remains, from the bitterness of what will never be,
The rapid calligraphy of these verses –
Colonnade started towards the Impossible.
But at least I dedicate to myself a contempt without tears,
Noble at least in the big gesture with which I throw
The dirty laundry I am – no list – into the course of things
And stay at home without a shirt.

(You, who console, who don't exist and therefore console,
Either Greek goddess, conceived as a statue that might be alive,
Or Roman matron, impossibly noble and wicked,
Or troubadours' princess, most gentle and bright vision,
Or eighteenth-century marquise, décolletée and distant,
Or celebrated cocotte of one's father's time,
Or something modern – I've no very clear idea what – ,
Be any of this whatever, and, if it can inspire, let it!
My heart is an overturned bucket.
Like the people who invoke spirits invoke spirits I invoke
Myself and meet with nothing.
I go to the window and see the street with absolute clarity:
I see the shops, I see the pavements, I see the traffic passing,
I see the living creatures in clothes, their paths crossing,
I see the dogs also existing,
And all this weighs on me like a sentence to banishment,
And all this is foreign, as all is.)

I have lived, have studied, have loved, and even believed,
And today there is not a beggar I do not envy simply for not being
me.

I look at each one's rags and ulcers and lying,
And I think: perhaps you never lived or studied or loved or believed
(Because it is possible to do the reality of all that without doing any
of it);
Perhaps you have barely existed, like when a lizard's tail is cut off
And it is a tail short of its lizard squirmingly.

I have made of me what I had not the skill for,
And what I could make of me I did not make.
The fancy dress I put on was the wrong one.
They knew me at once for who I was not and I did not expose the
lie, and lost myself.
When I tried to take off the mask,
It was stuck to my face.
When I got it off and looked at myself in the glass,
I had already grown old.
I was drunk, was trying in vain to get into the costume I had not
taken off.
I left the mask and went to sleep in the cloakroom
Like a dog that is tolerated by the management
Because he is harmless
And here I am, on the point of writing this story to prove I am
sublime.

Musical essence of my useless verses,
If only I could meet with you as something of my own doing,
Instead of staying always facing the Tobacconist's opposite,
Trampling underfoot consciousness of existing,
Like a carpet that a drunk stumbles over
Or a doormat the gipsies stole and was worth nothing.

But the Lord of the Tobacco Store has come to the door and
stopped in the doorway.
I look at him with the unease of a head twisted askew
And the unease of a soul understanding askew.
He will die and I shall die.
He will leave the shop-sign, I shall leave verses.
At a certain stage the shop-sign also will die, and the verses also.

After a certain stage the street where the shop-sign was will die,
And the language the verses were written in.
Later will die the revolving planet on which all this took place.
On other satellites of other systems something like people
Will continue making things like verses and living under things like
                                                    shop-signs,
Always one thing opposite another,
Always one thing as useless as another,
Always the impossible as stupid as the real,
Always the underlying mystery as sure as the sleep of the surface
                                                    mystery,
Always this or always some other thing or neither one thing nor the
                                                    other.

But a man has gone into the Tobacconist's (to buy some tobacco?)
And plausible reality has descended suddenly over me.
I half rise energetic, convinced, human,
And resolve to write these verses in which I say the contrary.

I light a cigarette as I think of writing them
And I savour in the cigarette liberation from all thought.
I follow the smoke like a route of my own
And enjoy, for a sensitive and competent moment,
Liberation from all speculations
And awareness that metaphysics is a consequence of feeling out of
                                                    sorts.

Then I sink into my chair
And continue smoking.
As long as Destiny concedes it, I shall continue smoking.

(If I married the daughter of my laundress
Perhaps I would be happy.)

At this I get up from the chair. I go to the window.

The man has come out of the Tobacconist's (putting change into
                                        his trousers pocket?)
Ah, I know him; it's Steve, he has no metaphysics.
(The Lord of the Tobacco Store has come to the door.)
As if by some divine instinct Steve has turned and has seen me.

He has waved me a greeting, I have shouted to him *Adeus ó Estéves*,
                                                                and the universe
Has rebuilt me itself without ideal or hope, and the Lord of the
                                                Tobacconist's has smiled.

15.1.1928
Álvaro de Campos

Translated by Jonathan Griffin

HAROLD PINTER

The Irish Shape

Not for this am I for nothing here,
But for that only I remain from her.
But for that only I should close the day,
Let the sky trade with the other skull,
But for that only and the Irish shape.
Not for this nothing do I frown this hand,
Not for this sunlight and the cage I am,
Only for this mirror and this all spring's time,
Only for the passing of the sea below,
Only for the silence, for her eyebrow.

1951

I know the place

I know the place.
It is true.
Everything we do
Corrects the space
Between death and me
And you.

1975

Cancer Cells

Cancer cells are those which have forgotten how to die
Nurse, Royal Marsden hospital

They have forgotten how to die
And so extend their killing life.

I and my tumour dearly fight.
Let's hope a double death is out.

I need to see my tumour dead
A tumour which forgets to die
But plans to murder me instead.

But I remember how to die
Though all my witnesses are dead.
But I remember what they said
Of tumours which would render them
As blind and dumb as they had been
Before the birth of that disease
Which brought the tumour into play.

The black cells will dry up and die
Or sing with joy and have their way.
They breed so quietly night and day,
You never know, they never say.

2002

PO CHÜ-I

Song and Dance

In Ch'ang-an the year draws to its close;
A great snow fills the Royal Domain.
And through the storm, on their way back from Court,
In reds and purples the dukes and barons ride.
They can enjoy the beauty of wind and snow;
To the rich they do not mean hunger and cold.
At a grand entry coaches and riders press;
Candles are lit in the Tower of Dance and Song.
Delighted guests pack knee to knee;
Heated with wine they throw off their double furs.
The host is high in the Board of Punishments;
The chief guest comes from the Ministry of Justice.
It was broad daylight when the drinking and music began;
Midnight has come, and still the feast goes on.
What do they care that at Wên-hsiang to-night
In the town gaol prisoners are freezing to death?

The Chrysanthemums in the Eastern Garden

AD 812

The days of my youth left me long ago;
And now in their turn dwindle my years of prime.
With what thoughts of sadness and loneliness
I walk again in this cold, deserted place!
In the midst of the garden long I stand alone;
The sunshine, faint; the wind and dew chill.
The autumn lettuce is tangled and turned to seed;
The fair trees are blighted and withered away.
All that is left are a few chrysanthemum-flowers

That have newly opened beneath the wattled fence.
I had brought wine and meant to fill my cup,
When the sight of these made me stay my hand.
                    I remember, when I was young,
How quickly my mood changed from sad to gay.
If I saw wine, no matter at what season,
Before I drank it, my heart was already glad.
                    But now that age comes
A moment of joy is harder and harder to get.
And always I fear that when I am quite old
The strongest liquor will leave me comfortless.
Therefore I ask you, late chrysanthemum-flower,
At this sad season why do you bloom alone?
Though well I know that it was not for my sake,
Taught by you, for a while I will smooth my frown.

Translated by Arthur Waley

ROBERT M. POLLET

Egyptian Child

Egyptian child do not cry now
In the hollow centre of the night;
Do not cry, all hurt children
Cry, but do not cry, your
Mother is near and your
Father is there, and angels low –
Beamed on shafts of moonlight
Gather round your bed in maritime rhythm,
To glow about your head and show
You all future protection now,
As I toss on my bed seeing my children.

JOHN PRESS

Womanisers

Adulterers and customers of whores
And cunning takers of virginities
Caper from bed to bed, but not because
The flesh is pricked to infidelities.

The body is content with homely fare;
It is the avid, curious mind that craves
New pungent sauce and strips the larder bare,
The palate and not hunger that enslaves.

Don Juan never was a sensualist:
Scheming fresh triumphs, artful, wary, tense,
He took no pleasure in the breasts he kissed
But gorged his ravenous mind and starved each sense.

An itching, tainted intellectual pride
Goads the salt lecher till he has to know
Whether all women's eyes grow bright and wide,
All wives and whores and virgins shudder so.

Hunters of women burn to show their skill,
Yet when the panting quarry has been caught
Mere force of habit drives them to the kill:
The soft flesh is less savoury than their sport.

The Shadows

After forty the shadows start to fall.
I think of a few friends
On whom the encroaching darkness descends.

There was one who stared for hours at a wall,
Lying on an iron bed,
With a weight lurching about in his head.

Another, plunging into alcohol,
Found it as bitter as
The lees of sex, the soured wine of the Mass.

A third gulped down fistfuls of seconal
But was still not granted
The long sleep that he had always wanted.

A stomach pump dredged him; a hospital
Passed six shocks through his brain;
A good psychiatrist tried to explain

The root of his trouble was Oedipal.
Though he still cannot sleep
He has some inkling of what makes him weep.

Our own darkness shelters daimons who call
Till we take the long spiral
Down to a stifling, self-created hell.

I too have watched the shadows growing tall.
May light perpetual
Shine on the haunted and redeem us all.

Neighbours

He is pretty pleased with himself tonight,
Posted on the oak, this father-to-be,
King of blackbirds whose golden repertoire
Claims my garden as his territory.

Twenty yards away, hidden behind claws
Of breaking magnolia and a veil
Of midges yoyoing before bedtime,
His mate sits tight, her immaculate nest

Glued to the trellis-work fence. Earlier
I had lumbered from the house, a giant
Whose shadow threatened to eclipse the sun
And sent her scuttling into sanctuary.

For precious seconds she kept to a bush
Knowing that her present of freckled eggs
Delivered at Easter, lay waiting
To be clutched again in her warm embrace.

But she dared not stir until the menace,
Now guiltily aware of his trespass,
Manhandled his bicycle from a shed
And, to her relief, trundled out of view.

This evening the waste-paper bin begs
To be emptied but from the kitchen window
I see a head and beak aimed towards me
Like a soldier crouched behind a bunker.

She shifts slightly, suspecting every move,
And in the tiny target of her eye
Terror and tenderness are liquefied.
I tiptoe back, not daring to go out,

And concede her advantage of the day,
Recognizing her right to share this place,
Content to listen while her sentry sends
A billet-doux before the last light has gone.

SALLY PURCELL

Guenever and the looking-glass

Repeated windows and walls of light
pour down to an invisible sun,
centre of all colonnades of nightmare;
full moon can raise no ghost now,
no flood follow this ebb-tide,
the brightness lies on a gleaned field.
I would not ever understand
why the Quest must claim you –
all it ever did was kill, dazzle,
maim or madden – you did not need
to follow that. I thought you
an opal from Lucifer's crown.

March 1603

The tapestry shivers like a candle-flame
in that little wind cold as a serpent
that creeps from the grave;
the table is a dark river
reflecting silver gleams
that draw night nearer.

An old woman, dying, keeps a sword by her bed
that none dare say, The Queen is afraid,
stabs repeatedly at woven god & hunter
– or the turbulent ghosts behind them –
while their fragile figures move
through her constant looking-glass.

One night she saw her body
'lean and fearful in a light of fire';
her spirit already walks corridors
where her dead are whispering;
only they can say 'must' to princes,
and she will not ward them off much longer.

HENRY REED

The Auction Sale

Within the great grey flapping tent
The damp crowd stood or stamped about;
And some came in, and some went out
To drink the moist November air;
None fainted, though a few looked spent
And eyed some empty unbought chair.
It was getting on. And all had meant
Not to go home with empty hands
But full of gain, at little cost,
Of mirror, vase, or vinaigrette.
Yet often, after certain sales,
Some looked relieved that they had lost,
Others, at having won, upset.
Two men from London sat apart,
Both from the rest and each from each,
One man in grey and one in brown.

And each ignored the other's face,
And both ignored the endless stream
Of bed and bedside cabinet.
They gazed intent upon the floor,
And both were strangers in that place.

Two other men, competing now,
Locals, whom everybody knew,
In shillings genially strove
For some small thing in ormolu.
Neither was eager; one looked down
Blankly at eighty-four, and then
Rallied again at eighty-eight,
And took it off at four pound ten.
The loser grimly shook his fist,
But friendly, there was nothing meant.
Little gained was little missed,
And there was smiling in the tent.

The auctioneer paused to drink,
And wiped his lips and looked about,
And held in whispered colloquy
The clerk, who frowned and seemed to think,
And murmured: 'Why not do it next?'
The auctioneer, though full of doubt,
Unacquiescent, rather vexed,
At last agreed, and at his sign
Two ministrants came softly forth
And lifted in an ashen shroud
Something extremely carefully packed,
Which might have been some sort of frame,
And was a picture-frame in fact.
They steadied it gently and with care,
And held it covered, standing there.

The auctioneer again looked round
And smiled uneasily at friends,
And said: 'Well, friends, I have to say
Something I have not said today:
There's a reserve upon this number.
It is a picture which though unsigned
Is thought to be of the superior kind,

So I am sure you gentlemen will not mind
If I tell you at once, before we start,
That what I have been asked to say
Is, as I have said, to say:
There's a reserve upon this number.
There was a rustle in that place,
And some awoke as though from slumber.
Anxious disturbance fluttered there;
And as if summoned to begin,
Those who had stepped outside for air
Retrieved themselves, and stepped back in.

The ministrants, two local boys,
Experienced in this sort of work,
And careful not to make too much noise,
Reached forward to unhook the shroud
That slowly opening fell away
And on the public gaze released
The prospect of a great gold frame
Which through the reluctant leaden air
Flashed a mature unsullied grace
Into the faces of the crowd.
And there was silence in that place.

> *Effulgent in the Paduan air,*
> *Ardent to yield the Venus lay*
> *Naked upon the sunwarmed earth.*
> *Bronze and bright and crisp her hair,*
> *By the right hand of Mars caressed,*
> *Who sunk beside her on his knee,*
> *His mouth toward her mouth inclined,*
> *His left hand near her silken breast.*
> *Flowers about them sprang and twined,*
> *Accomplished Cupids leaped and sported,*
> *And three, with dimpled arms enlaced*
> *And brimming gaze of stifled mirth,*
> *Looked wisely on at Mars's nape,*
> *While others played with horns and pikes,*
> *Or smaller objects of like shape.*

And there was silence in that place.
They gazed in silence; silently

The wind dropped down, no longer shook
The flapping sides and gaping holes.
And some moved back, and others went
Closer, to get a better look.

> *In ritual, amorous delay,*
> *Venus deposed her sheltering hand*
> *Where her bright belly's aureate day*
> *Melted to dusk about her groin;*
> *And, as from words that Mars had said*
> *Into that hidden, subtle ear,*
> *She turned away her shining head.*

The auctioneer cleared his throat,
And said: 'I am sure I'm right in feeling
You will not feel it at all unfair
For what when all is said and done
Is a work of very artistic painting
And not to be classed with common lumber,
And anyway extremely rare,
You will not feel it at all unfair
If I mention again before proceeding,
There's a reserve upon this number.
Someone was clearly heard to say:
'What, did I hear him say *reserve?*'
(Meaning, of course, a different meaning.)
This was a man from Sturminster,
Renowned for a quiet sense of fun,
And there was laughter in that place,
Though not, of course, from everyone.

> *A calm and gentle mile away,*
> *Among the trees a river ran*
> *Boated with blue and scarlet sails;*
> *A towered auburn city stood*
> *Beyond them on the burnished heights,*
> *And afar off and over all*
> *The azure day for mile on mile*
> *Uncoiled towards the Dolomites.*

The auctioneer said:
'I very much fear I have to say

I'm afraid we cannot look all day.
The reserve is seven hundred pounds.
Will anyone offer me seven fifty?
Seven thirty? Twenty-five?
Thank you, sir. Seven twenty-five.'
It was the man in brown who nodded,
Soon to be joined by him in grey.
The bidding started quietly.
No one from locally joined in.
Left to the men from London way,
The auctioneer took proper pride,
And knew the proper way to guide
By pause, by silence, and by tapping,
The bidding towards a proper price.
And each of the two with unmoved face
Would nod and pause and nod and wait.
And there was tension in that place.

    And still within the Paduan field,
    The silent summer scene stood by,
    The sails, the hill-tops, and the sky,
    And the bright warmth of Venus' glance
    That had for centuries caught the eye
    Of whosoever looked her way,
    And now caught theirs, on this far day.

Two people only did not look.
They were the men so calmly nodding,
Intently staring at the floor;
Though one of them, the one in brown,
Would sometimes slowly lift his gaze
And stare up towards the canvas roof,
Whereat a few men standing near
Inquiring eyes would also raise
To try to see what he was seeing.
The bidding mounted steadily
With silent nod or murmured yes
And passed the fifteen hundred mark,
And well beyond, and far beyond,
A nodding strife without success,
Till suddenly, with one soft word,
Something unusual occurred.

The auctioneer had asked politely,
With querying look and quiet smile:
'Come then, may I say two thousand?'
There was the customary pause,
When suddenly, with one soft word,
Another voice was strangely heard
To join in, saying plainly: 'Yes.'
Not their voices, but a third.
Everyone turned in some surprise
To look, and see, and recognize
A young man who some time ago
Had taken a farm out Stalbridge way,
A very pleasant young man, but quiet,
Though always a friendly word to say,
Though no one in the dealing line,
But quiet and rather unsuccessful,
And often seen about the place
At outings or on market day,
And very polite and inoffensive,
And *quiet*, as anyone would tell you,
But not from round here in any case.

The auctioneer, in some surprise,
Said: 'Please, sir, did I hear you say
Yes to two thousand? Is that bid?
Twenty hundred am I bid?'
The two were silent, and the third,
The young man, answered plainly: 'Yes.
Yes. Two thousand. Yes, I did.'
Meaning that he had said that word.
'Ah, yes. Yes, thank you, sir,' concurred
The auctioneer, surprised, but glad
To know that he had rightly heard,
And added: 'Well, then, I may proceed.
I am bid two thousand for this picture.
Any advance upon that sum?
Any advance upon two thousand?
May I say two thousand twenty?
Twenty? Thirty? Thank you, sir.
May I say forty? Thank you, sir.
Fifty? You, sir? Thank you, sir.'

And now instead of two, the three
Competed in the bargaining.
There was amazement in that place,
But still it gave, as someone said,
A sort of interest to the thing.
The young man nodded with the others,
And it was seen his nice young face,
Had lost its flush and now was white,
And those who stood quite near to him
Said (later, of course, they did not speak
While the bidding was going on)
That on his brow were beads of sweat,
Which as he nodded in acceptance
Would, one or two, fall down his cheek.
And in the tightening atmosphere
Naked upon the sunwarmed earth
Pauses were made and eyebrows raised,
Answered at last by further nods,
Ardent to yield the nods resumed
Venus upon the sunwarmed nods
Abandoned Cupids danced and nodded
His mouth towards her bid four thousand
Four thousand, any advance upon,
And still beyond four thousand fifty
Unrolled towards the nodding *sun*.

But it was seen, and very quickly,
That after four thousand twenty-five,
The man from over Stalbridge way
Did not respond, and from that point
He kept his silent gaze averted,
To show he would not speak again.
And it was seen his sweating face,
Which had been white, was glowing red,
And had a look almost of pain.

> *Oh hand of Venus, hand of Mars.*
> *Oh ardent mouth, oh burnished height,*
> *Oh blue and scarlet gentle sails,*
> *Oh Cupids smiling in the dance,*
> *Oh unforgotten, living glance,*
> *Oh river, hill and flowering plain,*
> *Oh ever-living dying light*

He had a look almost of pain.
The rest was quickly done. The bids
Advanced at slowly slackening pace
Up to four thousand eighty-five.
And at this point the man in grey
Declined his gaze upon the floor
And kept it there, as though to say
That he would bid no more that day.
It was quite clear he had not won,
This man in grey, though anyone
Practised to read the human face
Might on his losing mouth descry
What could no doubt be termed a smile.
While on the face of him in brown
A like expertness might discern
Something that could be termed a frown.

There was a little faint applause.

The auctioneer sighed with joy,
The customary formalities
Were quickly over, and the strangers
Nodding a brief goodbye departed.
Venus and Mars were carefully veiled.
The auctioneer went on and proffered
Vase and table, chair and tray.
Bids of a modest kind were offered,
The traffic of a normal day.
A little later it was seen
The young man too had slipped away.
Which was, of course, to be expected.
Possibly there was nothing else
There at the sale to take his fancy.
Or possibly he even might
Be feeling ashamed at intervening,
Though possibly not, for after all,
He had certainly been within his right.

At all events, an hour later,
Along the Stalbridge road a child
Saw the young man and told her mother,
Though not in fact till some days after,

That she had seen him in the dusk,
Not walking on the road at all,
But striding beneath the sodden trees;
And as she neared she saw that he
Had no covering on his head,
And did not seem to see her pass,
But went on, through the soaking grass,
Crying. That was what she said.

Bitterly, she later added.

Crying bitterly, she said.

1956

JAMES REEVES

The Little Brother

God! how they plagued his life, the three damned sisters,
Throwing stones at him out of the cherry trees,
Pulling his hair, smudging his exercises,
Whispering. How passionately he sees
His spilt minnows flounder in the grass.

There will be sisters subtler far than these,
Baleful and dark, with slender, cared-for hands,
Who will not smirk and babble in the trees,
But feed him with sweet words and provocations,
And in his sleep practise their sorceries,
Appearing in the form of ragged clouds
And at the corners of malignant seas.

As with his wounded life he goes alone
To the world's end, where even tears freeze,
He will in bitter memory and remorse
Hear the lost sisters innocently tease.

The Prisoners

Somehow we never escaped
    Into the sunlight,
Though the gates were always unbarred
    And the warders tight.
For the sketches on the walls
    Were to our liking,
And squeaks from the torture-cell
    Most satisfying.

ANNE RIDLER

A Matter of Life and Death

I did not see the iris move,
I did not feel the unfurling of my love.

This was the sequence of the flower:
First the leaf from which the bud would swell,
No prison, but a cell,
A rolled rainbow;
Then the sheath that enclosed the blow
Pale and close
Giving no hint of the blaze within,
A tender skin with violet vein.
Then the first unfurling petal

As if a hand that held a jewel
Curled back a finger, let the light wink
Narrowly through the chink,
Or like the rays before the sunrise
Promising glory.

And while my back is turned, the flower has blown.
Impossible to tell
How this opulent blossom from that spick bud has grown.
The chrysalis curled tight,
The flower poised for flight –
Corolla with lolling porphyry wings
And yellow tiger markings
A chasing-place for shade and light:
Between these two, the explosion
Soundless, with no duration.
      (I did not see the iris move,
      I did not feel my love unfurl.)
The most tremendous change takes place in silence,
Unseen, however you mark the sequence,
Unheard, whatever the din of exploding stars.

Down the porphyry stair
Headlong into the air
The boy has come: he crouches there
A tender startled creature
With a fawn's ears and hair-spring poise
Alert to every danger
Aghast at every noise.
A blue blink
From under squeezed-up lids
As mauve as iris buds
Is gone as quickly as a bird's bright wink.
Gone – but as if his soul had looked an instant through the chink.
And perfect as his shell-like nails,
Close as are to the flower its petals,
My love unfolded with him.
Yet till this moment what was he to me?
Conjecture and analogy;
Conceived, and yet unknown;
Behind this narrow barrier of bone
Distant as any foreign land could be.

I have seen the light of day,
Was it sight or taste or smell?
What I have been, who can tell?
What I shall be, who can say?

He floats in life as a lily in the pool
Free and yet rooted;
And strong though seeming frail,
Like the ghost fritillary
That trails its first-appearing bud
As though too weak to raise it from the mud,
But is stronger than you dream,
And soon will lift its paper lantern
High upon an arched and sinewy stem.

His smiles are all largesse,
Need ask for no return,
Since give and take are meaningless
To one who gives by needing
And takes our love for granted
And grants a favour even by his greed.
The ballet of his twirling hands
His chirping and his loving sounds,
Perpetual expectation
Perpetual surprise –
Not a lifetime satisfies
For watching, everything he does
We wish him to do always.

Only in a lover's eyes
Shall I be so approved again;
Only the other side of pain
Can truth again be all I speak,
Or I again possess
A saint's hilarious carelessness.

He rows about his ocean
With its leaning cliffs and towers,
A horizontal being,
Straddled by walking people
By table-legs and chairs;
And sees the world as you can see

Upside-down in water
The wavering heights of trees
Whose roots hang from your eyes.
Then Time begins to trail
In vanishing smoke behind him,
A vertical creature now
With a pocket full of nails,
One of a gang of urchin boys
Who proves his sex by robber noise –
Roar of the sucking dove
And thunder of the wren.
Terror waits in the woods
But in the sun he is brazen
Because our love is his
No matter what he does;
His very weakness claims a share
In the larger strength of others,
And perfect in our eyes
He is only vulnerable there.

But not immortal there, alas.
We cannot keep, and see. The shapes of clouds
Which alter as we gaze
Are not more transient than these living forms
Which we so long to hold
For ever in the moment's mould.
The figures frozen in the camera's record
And carried with us from the past
Are like those objects buried with the dead –
Temporal treasures irrelevant to their need.
Yes, this is the worst:
The living truth is lost,
And is supplanted by these album smiles.

> *What you desire to keep, you slay:*
> *While you watch me, I am going.*
> *Wiser than you, I would not stay*
> *Even if I could: my hope's in growing.*
> *My form as a dapple of sun that flies*
> *On the brook, is changed; my earliest word*
> *Is the call you learnt to recognize*
> *And now forget, of a strange bird.*

Yet, as the calyx contains the life of the bud
So the bud is contained within the flower
Though past in time:
The end is not more true than the beginning,
Nor is the promise cancelled by the prime.
Not only what he was, and is, but what he might have been,
In each is rolled within.
Our life depends on that:
What other claim have we to resurrection?
For now that we can contemplate perfection
We have lost the knack of being it. What should be saved
Of these distorted lives?
All we can pray is
                            Save us from Nothingness.
Nothingness, which all men dread;
Which makes us feel an irrational pity for the dead,
And fight the anodyne
Even while we long for deliverance from pain.

So, I have read,
When a man gave his darling in grief to the grave
About her neck in a locket tied
He set this urgent word –
Not to drink Lethe, at all costs not to forget.
And this is truth to us, even yet.
For if life is eternal
All must be held, though all must be redeemed.
But what can ever restore
To these sad and short-coming lives of ours
The lovely jocund creatures that we were
And did not know we were?
What can give us at once
The being and the sense?

Why, each within
Has kept his secret for some Resurrection:
The wonder that he was
And can be, which is his
Not by merit, only by grace.
It comes to light, as love is born with a child,
Neither with help nor herald
(I did not see the iris move);
Neither by sight nor sound –
I did not feel the unfurling of my love.

Angel of Harwich

She was usually good for a fuck
If she liked you, or just felt
Like a change from long hours
At the bar at the mercy of bores –
She'd flick you a look, then turn on her heel,
Legs in black nylon the colour of rail,
Making for the shed by the siding
That backed on the quay. Soon you would feel
The hardening thrust of those low-sliding
Breasts as she pressed and then knelt
As she liked and bucked as you felt
She was starting to come. She'd wail
Gently, straighten and then tuck
Her blouse back into her skirt, kiss,
And, slightly unsteady, trot her way back,
Humming. You marvelled at your luck.

Better than to scorn is to bless
Such promiscuity, the 'angel of Harwich'
Who made love as a nurse
Might minister to the suffering, eyes
And legs wide, but with so rich,
So tender a compassion only fools would despise.
At sea, it was her you'd most miss.

Clothes on a Chair

Waking, she saw on the chair
The clothes of the man beside her,
Trousers, shirt, vest untidily spilled,
But into a shape that was vaguely human;
And being that kind of woman,
Asked herself what kind of man filled
Them, a question she could not answer.

Leave Train

Yellow as daffodils as wax fingers
Yellow as death as a mandarin
Rosyth with eyes like a stranger
Rosyth with the pallor of dawn.

Shunting of engines in sky torn
Like a curtain, shunting of objects
In memories divested of features.
Without you without you without you

The bell of the blood in a deep sea
Drowns, the hood of the face is eyeless.
An emptied body in a warm room
An emptied body in its own tomb.

Dawn tricked out with sick stars
Dawn curdled with smoke
Yellow as fog as this compartment
Yellow as dogs' eyes as a death's head.

Without you without you without you
Branches are naked and wracked with fever
Rosyth is a terminus evil as an adder
Rosyth is absence that goes on forever

Yellow as dead flowers as a shared south
Yellow as desire as face to face
Dawn with a handful of spare hours
Dawn with hangover and a taste in the mouth.

MARTIN SEYMOUR-SMITH

On the Beach

Here where the sea licks
Still unvanished stone
I maul my mind
With how I wronged your innocence
And can no more than plead
As the world is ground
Away: rescue me, rescue me,
Angel of the matchless voice,
Teach me true desire.

Learning to Fall Out of Love

What, dear one, had you to do
With my lengthless evenings
Of distressed unmiracle?
You like less than most
To cause any heart to ache
And when I told you I loved you
I know I saw anger
In the way your eyes turned –
Even though their undimmed depths

Were as indifferent to me
As are all shimmering seas
To distant ships which send, unceasingly,
Dejected signals to the ports.

You did nothing. But in an instant
You became the one for whom I yearned
And I lost all I'd ever learned.

Yet if the loved one's perfect,
Which my heart told me was fact,
It must have been a lie:
Quel âme est sans défauts?

But I knew you were that ghost —
A glimpse of what, how near?
A snatch of words from where? —
I'd seen and heard upon the stair
At times of omen in my past:
Transmuted now to flesh and blood,
And with me in my life at last.
So quickly had you passed before,
So intermittently,
That you could be perfect for
It might have been a dream...

What now was I to make of it?
You as vulnerable as I
And scolding me for not
Being *critical enough.*

Somehow the jester beauty,
Vexed by its own sap,
Drove me into trespass,
For then it was I sought
To lead you from your living self
As though you still were ghost.

So I have learned to leave my loving,
Since that is your request,
Nor have I hopes of finding in your look
A shred of interest.

But my persistent heart insists
This cannot be the end:
I have already undertaken
An unexpected, dangerous voyage
Into your shimmering, lonely seas
That are so deep yet nonchalant –
So I give you my gratitude
For whatever fate may bring:
Whether I drown alone
Or return perhaps from hence
With cargoes now unknown,
I shall die, or I shall mend,
With courage I have found
Not in any phantom woman
But in your redolence.

C.H. SISSON

'If love and death are one and the same thing'

If love and death are one and the same thing,
As Ronsard said – others have felt it too –
Yet neither he nor they can make it true,
Nor anything, by mere imagining.
Whatever evidence the world may bring,
The mind fills like a pond and what looks through
The waters is the sky's cloud and blue,
But what have images to do with naming?
The names of love and death we have from far
But who can say what their originals are
Or whether the names they have are their own?
When we sail into that unexpected harbour
The moment of trespass beyond words is there,
All freshness and newness begin, or nothing is known.

For the Queen's Jubilee

What use in following
So many queens and kings,
Elizabeth of our spring,
Elizabeth of autumn now?

What use, unless you see
Music and poetry
Standing to your honour,
As we do now?

A coronation robe
May run in holes;
The Koh-in-Noor be sold
To pay the grocer:

But there were Muses once
– Muses, what do I say?
In the language of today,
Things which affront:

The severe line the draughtsman traces
Whether anyone likes it or not;
The clearly expressed thought
Which takes the smile off people's faces:

These are the Muses, it is these
Which call for no man's protection;
These it is which will be free
Against any venal objection:

It is these, too, which can save
Your reign in memory;
Your sceptre, your sway
Still live, for poetry.

Ellick Farm

The larks flew up like jack-in-the-boxes
From my moors, and the fields were edged with foxgloves.

The farm lay neatly within the hollow
The gables climbing, the barn beside the doorway.

If I had climbed into the loft I should have found a boy
Forty years back, among the bales of hay.

He would have known certainly all that I know
Seeing it in the muck-strewn cobbles below.

(Under the dark rim of the near wood
The tears gathered as under an eyelid.)

It would have surprised him to see a tall man
Who had travelled far, pretending to be him.

But that he should have been turning verses, half dumb
After half a lifetime, would least have surprised him.

Slightly Rhyming Verses for Jeff Bernard's Fiftieth Birthday

My dear Jeff,
I can't say enough
how much I admire
the way you have
conducted your entire
life, and the way you have
used your marvellous Muse.
And how right she was to
choose you. Because
she's a Rare Bird who would
have retired or died
if you hadn't known how
to amuse
her, and her you.
That's one non-bogus
marriage made
on Parnassus
and *true*.

She knew
exactly what and who
she was letting herself
in for: the real You.
Drink, betting shops and pubs
are the sort of thing that rubs
her up the right way:
she'll always stay
and make you more beautiful
and witty
every day.

This is a loose love
Ode, owed

to one of my friends
who is in my special
collection of people
who make amends
for endless excruciating
boring hours
so often lived
when foolishly pursuing
stimulation,
and none occurs.

Sterne, Benchley, Leacock,
Carroll, and Nash, and Lear
are not more dear
to me than bedrock
Bernard (3).
(Do I not pay 65p.
ungrudgingly weekly,
for a fixative laugh,
uniquely Jeff?,
who has become
a consolatory
addictive to me?)

Wilde would have smiled
and been beguiled
and bright enough to know
that *you* had a better
Muse in tow
than he.
Could he see
the angelic emanations
from gutters where we
all fall, while
trying to pee,
and rise, or try to rise,
unwisely, in majesty?

And Swift is bitter
and cross
and doesn't make us
feel better

at bearing our lot,
and, in his rage
at the odds,
misses the old adage
that recurs to me
often, in every mess:
'against stupidity
even the gods
are helpless.'
He
lifted furious fists
but had no effect
on the jibbering idjits.

Your subject is not mean,
who's up, who's in,
or jockeying for position
(what a dreary sin).
Funny but kind,
your subject is justly seen
as the inexhaustible one
of nude mankind:
Yourself, in fact, drinking,
amidst the alien corn,
and explaining the amazing joke
of being born.

Your sources –
grief and love
and the Coach & Horses
and all the things we're
thinking of
but don't admit,
because they don't fit
our grand ideas of
our own importance.
You hit the
soul on the head
when it rises
out of its lying bed,
pompous with portents
above its station,

and greedy for rewards
above its ration.

But you're never snide,
and you never hurt,
and you wouldn't want to win
on a doctored beast,
and anyhow the least
of your pleasures
resides in paltry measures.

So guard, great joker God, please guard
this great Bernard,
and let 1982
be the most brilliant year he ever knew.
Let him be known
for the prince of men he is,
a master at taking out of
himself and us the piss.

If you will do this, God,
I'll be good all year,
and try to be better-dressed,
and soberer, and keep my prose-style clear,
(for this great man
is embedded in my heart)
I'll remain, Sir, then and only then,
Yours sincerely, Elizabeth Smart.

Structures of Cancer

I *Disorders*

It starts with one: one cell, one string
untuned. The cell divides. The king
is usurped, degree is taken away.
Multiplication multiplies.
Kin with kin and kind with kind
are confounded. Augurers find
hard fact compacted in the entrails
of the chicken killed at sunrise.
The land riots. Fathers and sons
fight each other till the blood runs
cold in recognition and
only the survivor cries
out. Out in the foreign fen
in the mists other men,
purposive men, move, with other
kinds of recognising eyes.
They squint into the rising sun,
pray and joke together, gun
the blue-steel motors, check their maps
and their anti-Cong supplies.
Both kinds of men perceive
this fact to be hard: no reprieve,
when the string's untuned, for those
who will not hear. Nor fever-flies,
nor the magic dragon in his
lonely fen indulge in any
nice distinction. They kill us
for their random sport.

                    The wise
man welcomes *the first silent touch*
of chancre. After such pain such
a mainline brotherhood at last.

A life worth leaving is the prize.
The cell divides and the king dies..

II *From* The Times

There is no disease of cancer, but
a great many variable growth disorders.
Surfaces which come in contact with
the outside world, liable to induce
repeated growth demand, are most at risk.
Phenomena of learning, memory,
self-recognition, and the apparently
purposive carriage of information at
cellular and molecular levels:
such mechanisms, I read, *may confer*
immunity. Cancer victims tend
to have poor emotional outlets. Each
cell carries a great capacity for expression.

III *Capital*

Number 18 Cornwallis Crescent had stood
derelict two years, often changing hands
in polished offices elsewhere. We could
not raise a loan, and derelict it stands.

Mr Adams said the bank could not see its way.
It wasn't as though we had what I might call
security, he regretted having to say.
For capital growth, security was essential.

We broke in to look at what we hadn't got.
There was a monster growing on the pantry shelf.
A head-sized orange pustule of dry rot
had spored three more. The house was at war with itself.

*

The dhow takes gold for Vishnu
from Dubai to Bombay.

Vishnu has hashish
to ship back the next day.
East and West exchange
dream for dream as pay.

*

I heard once of a man who robbed a bank
and ran through the Bombay streets, until they caught him,
blossoming banknotes around him, fistful on fistful.
I imagine him gladder than he'd ever been,
seeing them trickle, lodge in sterile fissures.
His was a unique talent that flowered once.
I do not think his motive altered his sentence.

IV *Spores*

The usurer mushroom grows overnight, implants
its spores in generations, and imprints
its primary shadow on the frustrate earth.
Puffball is a magic dragon's breath.
The truffle is a sickness of the oak.
Tumours that seem healed may sprout after shock.

Physics lately told us that we were
to look at atomic parity askance.
O chestnut tree, diseased blossomer,
how can we tell your cancer from the chance?

V *Deviants*

If the growth is capital, the king dies:
shot, perhaps, riding through the street,
or murdered in his cell. All sick men are kings,
tyrants of the well-tucked sheet,
acting out what could not find a stage
in the whole world. The medical commissar
cures the deviant symptoms back into line,
and does not ask what the motives are.

If it is the body, not the head,
that conceives, the pain is acted out
anatomically. In such a state
any limb must serve as a redoubt
where power may regroup and find expression
partially. Those which are not sick
will be infiltrated, spied on, thought
alien to the body politic.

VI *Images*

The Times says we are in error, *ignorance, fear,*
superstition and expectation of magic
if we have an abnormal fear of cancer.
Such attitudes are *an affront to human reason.*
I read another report that said *the cancer*
problem needs an entirely new image.
Beat cancer and enjoy life eternal.
Play down Claude Debussy, who had a great
capacity for expression, and died of cancer.
The *Sunday Times* found cancer a good excuse
to print a naked breast, in purplish colours,
like a motor ad on some other page.

Your thinking might start: coffins are to us
what bastard children were to the Victorians.

No one marches to Trafalgar Square
against cancer.
No teach-ins, no party splits, no sessions chaired by Freddy
Grisewood, no self-immolated monks, no banned plays, no Rapacki
plans, no informed sources
about cancer.
If you want to suffer in the public domain
better make it a car smash, at Bank Holiday.

Which is the greater dignity: to die
laughing, or to go out sombre? And,
if laughing, at the stalking fate of it,
like some Hamlets, or the fortuitousness?
Another question: why do I bother to talk
to you, since we are both going to die?

Death is irrelevant. Chance is the beauty of cancer.
The fun of cancer is the fun of musical chairs.
The politics of cancer is a machine-gun playing
in the public square. Cancer's jurisprudence
is the second law of thermodynamics.
The substance of cancer is a hole that grows
in water. The shadow of cancer is one imprinted
when you move on. The charge of cancer is
positive, patrolled by negative police.

Cancer is a crab that bites in backwards,
a flower that shrinks back into its seed.
These are images of distraction. I
control them. They only move, only express.
What is ineradicably on your mind
is a good excuse, the last word in Webster.

Cancer kills a man but the idea saves him.

VII *Terms*

If I wrote down all those I knew
who died of cancer, what would it mean?
Credentials? Showing the wound? A somewhat pathetic
therapy for coming to terms with what is terminal?

My mother died of cancer. I do not
remember her. Ron Roberts had a tumour:
when they trepanned his skull he fought, they said,
remarkably to live. Tony Tillinghast,
twenty-nine then, like me, married, one child,
just got his PhD: the cloud first mushroomed
on his collarbone; what they didn't know,
as they civilly dealt with it, was that
the spores had fallen out all through his body.
I talked about cancer all one afternoon
(waiting to see a film from Vietnam)
with Charles Wood, when his mother-in-law
was ill. He wanted to find a way of coming
to terms with it, and tried to in a play:
when his seedy comic was seeking words

to express the love he felt for the wife he had played
hell with, he struggled and finally got it out,
I love you like cancer. I have known others,
as you have. What do you do with your names?
Have you got some technology of mourning?

VIII *Mainline*

Do not ask the brothers
for their reasons. They
are not reasonable.

Do not give them credit
cards. They have no interest.
Postdated honesty

is just Ben Franklin's tale.
Do not ask the brothers
for their story. They

are not narrative.
Their end is their beginning.
Their clocks do not shake hands.

As well invite the snail
to stretch his horns as ask
the brothers to extend

their brains in linear reason.
The long story of control
of earth, the dialectic

of men and minerals,
or discourse of respect, such
as Cézanne had with an apple,

are over for the brothers.
They have no messages
for the thing they are

become one gesture with.
The dust of consciousness
reverts to dust, blown

by whatever wind prevails,
along with Cézanne's apple,
and Ben Franklin's credit.

IX *Growth*

We all have cancer. Some
are victims, having to watch
the inexpressible conflict
clench and stumble toward us
across the lonely fen,
unrecognised but recognising men;
or having to act out
in the outside world
a dream, not studied but prompted
by memories not remembered.
If you would heal him, ask
the king what sweats behind his divine mask.
Knowledge is not enough,
alone, nor gesture. A whole man
wholly attends to all
he knows within himself,
and never ceases to grow;
even in death, become one with the slow
biochemistry of roots, and what roots know.

To Carry the Child

To carry the child into adult life
Is good? I say it is not,
To carry the child into adult life
Is to be handicapped.

The child in adult life is defenceless
And if he is grown-up, knows it,
And the grown-up looks at the childish part
And despises it.

The child, too, despises the clever grown-up,
The man-of-the-world, the frozen,
For the child has the tears alive on his cheek
And the man has none of them.

As the child has colours, and the man sees no
Colours or anything,
Being easy only in things of the mind,
The child is easy in feeling.

Easy in feeling, easily excessive
And in excess powerful,
For instance, if you do not speak to the child
He will make trouble.

You would say a man had the upper hand
Of the child, if a child survive,
I say the child has fingers of strength
To strangle the man alive.

Oh it is not happy, it is never happy,
To carry the child into adulthood,
Let children lie down before full growth
And die in their infanthood
And be guilty of no man's blood.

But oh the poor child, the poor child, what can he do,
Trapped in a grown-up carapace,
But peer outside of his prison room
With the eye of an anarchist?

BERNARD SPENCER

On the 'Sievering' Tram

Square figures climb off and on;
mufflers, Astrakhan hats.
A wintry night for a ride to a clinic
to visit a new-born boy and his mother;
and the bell hurrah-ing.

Too many life-bullied faces
packed on the Sievering tram.
Yet a woman smiles at a baby near her
and beckons and beckons, as we run lurch
-ing, and sigh and restart.

That baby views the woman steadily;
(and the floor is all mucked with snow.)
What do I bring to the boy and his mother
lying in the clinic? Daffodils,
bewilderment and love,

Ready money, a clock and a signature.
A Neon-light Pegasus glows in the sky
(Somebody's Oil) as we swing corners
past bakers' and laundries and snow, with the traffic
-gongs ringing like glory.

Part of Plenty

When she carries food to the table and stoops down
– Doing this out of love – and lays soup with its good
Tickling smell, or fry winking from the fire
And I look up, perhaps from a book I am reading
Or other work: there is an importance of beauty
Which can't be accounted for by there and then,
And attacks me, but not separately from the welcome
Of the food, or the grace of her arms.

When she puts a sheaf of tulips in a jug
And pours in water and presses to one side
The upright stems and leaves that you hear creak,
Or loosens them, or holds them up to show me,
So that I see the tangle of their necks and cups
With the curls of her hair, and the body they are held
Against, and the stalk of the small waist rising
And flowering in the shape of breasts;

Whether in the bringing of the flowers or the food
She offers plenty, and is part of plenty,
And whether I see her stooping, or leaning with the flowers,
What she does is ages old, and she is not simply,
No, but lovely in that way.

JON STALLWORTHY

War Poet

> *facilis descensus Averno:*
> *noctes atque dies patet atri ianua Ditis;*
> *sed revocare gradum superasque evadere ad auras,*
> *hoc opus, hic labor est.*
> Virgil, *Aeneid* VI, 126–9

Back to South Leigh for evensong
and, in the sermon, watched the long
arm of the sun restore the Doom
above the chancel arch. *Thy kingdom
come,* with a vengeance! The entrenched dead,
rising as Reveille sounded,
parted company. Sinners condemned
to join the chain-gang of the damned
recovered 'objects of desire'
and fell in for eternal fire.

I knew them, even naked – Smith,
Haynes, Adrian, Hill, Roberts (with
his hand restored) – my own lot, plus
the General. *He* had earned his place!
But then, herded with them downhill,
I was reprieved. Detailed for hell,
I heard beyond the traverse
an archangelic sentry's voice:
'Wiring party coming in.'
They came in without Adrian.

*

We never found him – never will –
with the 25-pounders still
pounding the waves of wire and mist.
We miss him in the morning most
when his Reveille, whistled, set

the blackbird on the parapet
Reveille-ing back
                    Did another
one whistle over Golgotha?

*

Are you still there – and still my love,
lighting a candle for me still?
I have been Absent Without Leave

almost from life itself, they tell
me, the good sisters, since Christophe
exhumed me from the house a shell

brought blazing down. The boy is deaf
and dumb, but lion-hearted! Hurt
his hands freeing me, dragging off

a burning rafter and the shirt
of Nessus. *St* Christophe saved me,
discovering a heart-beat, heart-

beat in the blackened turnip he
delivered to the convent door.
Dear love, I have no memory

of these things, *anything* before
the light, tidal not candle light.
I was dissolved in what I saw –

for days, months, centuries it might
have been. Until in God's good time
or timelessness, the tide of light

began to ebb and I to climb
to consciousness, to tidal pain.
That also ebbed in God's good time

to leave me stranded, eyes open,
seeing only distant sails
tacking through fog. It cleared, and then

I saw white coifs between the isles
of broken castaways. One night,
a coif and candle came from miles

away. Something about the white
hand holding the white candle set
a fuse behind the eyes alight.

Lying there, trying to forget
the bad dreams, suddenly I knew
that somewhere there was something yet

to live for. Fuselight led me through
my mined archives to a blaze
of recognition – nights and days with you.

                    *

Numbness and disbelief –
as Roberts in No Man's Land
felt, finding he had no hand
below a pumping sleeve.

Without you, I am learning
about death. It cannot be true
that you – you – you –
and my numbness turning

to anger. But however slow
the fire, however deep the seam,
it will burn out, they say, in time.
In time for what? Forgiveness? No.

Acceptance? How should I resign
myself to knowing that you lie
under another sky
in other arms than mine?

                    *

The bears you kept for company
sharing your bed when I could not,

the pair you christened You and Me –
our old Familiars – in what

new room do they keep company?
Your place or his place, and in what
position – bear or missionary?
Or are they banished to some spot

chillier than they used to know –
up on a shelf, facing the wall,
hearing no evil, seeing no
evil, speaking no evil at all?

Such delicacy I commend,
such reticence – but love is weak
and, lamentably, in the end
Orpheus will always turn and speak.

                    *

Heart, full as the moon
was full, a broken ring now,
an empty sky soon.

                    *

The things one remembers – a liking
for candles – *where* one remembers, and *why*.

Tuscany. A cracked clapper striking
the hour in a shimmering sky.

San Nicolò called me across the square
from sunlight to starlight, a glimmering
constellation of candles. Star-gazing there,
I lost – and found – myself remembering

candles beside our bed, cinnamon,
sandalwood spicing the air.
San Nicolò watched me light one
for you and might have heard a prayer:

If you should see her candles bloom
beside another bed that she
now shares, let her in an outer room
light one for me.

*

Back – for your wedding – to South Leigh.
The church was empty but for me
and overhead (as the saint says)
so great a cloud of witnesses.
Remember them? The Last Reveille
summoning sinners to the melée
at the mouth of hell?
                              Ached for the damned
that day as for myself, condemned
to witness what I hoped was joy:
vows, rings, exchanged; lips and hands joined
a world away. I should have sung
for you, but with my lyre unstrung
epithalamia were not
on hand. Instead, I wrote this note
by candle-light – one lit for you
and when it went out, I went too.

*

Whenever the child cried out at night,
he would be rescued by a blade of light,
a mother's paper and pencil. 'Draw
me the horror you say you saw,
and your drawing will drive it away.'
Your grown child heard that again today.

I was trying to escape, cutting a path
uphill in the sulphurous aftermath
of some Armageddon, sensed but not seen
in the valley where we had been.
No sound but the bark of a dog, somewhere
ahead or behind us, rasping the air
as we with our gasping, she and I.
Her voice then behind me: 'Look how the sky

lightens along the ridge. If we can keep
heading for that, who knows, we could sleep
in a happy valley.'
                    It was true –
the bright ridge a blade to the rescue.
I turned to take her hand, but as I did
her body, like a candle, melted
into smoke, a writhing ghost the wind
snatched from my arms.
                        Real or imagined
the animal cry that woke me? Hers
or mine? No exorcist answers
as I write this, and an Arctic light
uncovers the bedspread and the white
pillow warmed, through other nights, by one
whose smile was my sunrise. My un-
returning, subterranean sun.

                    *

You again, blackbird! Welcome back –
as you were welcomed to a white
window-sill in the labour ward,
welcoming me to my first light.

No inkling of the mistress you
would herald, when you piped us up
to No Man's Land. She found me words
to shield the firestep

under fire, and afterwards
to pull me back, scorched but alive,
from other fires. Why should I
be granted a ticket of leave

if not to honour her and learn
from you – singing through rain or sun
your Edensong, till a dark wind
blows out the chestnut candles, one

by one?

GASPARA STAMPA

'Love, standing by my side'

Love, standing by my side,
keeps saying to me, 'Poor girl,
what will your life be now he's gone,
who gave you such happiness?'
And I say, 'Why did you show him
to me that first time, there
for a moment and gone again,
if you only meant to kill me?'
Then he sees he is in the wrong
and says nothing, and I go on grieving,
my heart knows how piteously!
My prayers are no good, if I pray,
because I send them all to him
who cares little or nothing for my pain.

'All the planets in heaven, all the stars'

All the planets in heaven, all the stars,
gave my lord their graces at his conception;
all gave him their special gifts,
to make one perfect mortal man.
Saturn gave loftiness of understanding,
Jove the desire for noble deeds,
Mars more skill in war than any other,
Phoebus Apollo elegance and wit.
Venus gave him beauty and gentle ways,
Mercury eloquence; but the moon alone
made him too freezing cold for me.
Every one of these rare graces
makes me burn for his brilliant flame,
and one alone has turned him into ice.

Translated by Sally Purcell

Song

Honest lover whatsoever,
If in all thy love there ever
Was one wav'ring thought, if thy flame
Were not still even still the same:
     Know this,
     Thou lov'st amiss,
     And to love true,
Thou must begin again, and love anew.

If when she appears i' th' room,
Thou dost not quake, and are struck dumb,
And in striving this to cover,
Dost not speak thy words twice over,
     Know this,
     Thou lov'st amiss,
     And to love true,
Thou must begin again, and love anew.

If fondly thou dost not mistake,
And all defects for graces take,
Persuad'st thyself that jests are broken,
When she hath little or nothing spoken,
     Know this,
     Thou lov'st amiss,
     And to love true,
Thou must begin again, and love anew.

If when thou appearest to be within,
Thou lett'st not men ask and ask again;
And when thou answerest, if it be
To what was ask'd thee, properly,
     Know this,
     Thou lov'st amiss,
     And to love true,
Thou must begin again, and love anew.

If when thy stomach calls to eat,
Thou cutt'st not fingers 'stead of meat,
And with much gazing on her face
Dost not rise hungry from the place,
   Know this,
    Thou lov'st amiss,
    And to love true,
Thou must begin again, and love anew.

If by this thou dost discover
That thou art no perfect lover,
And desiring to love true,
Thou dost begin to love anew:
   Know this,
    Thou lov'st amiss,
    And to love true,
Thou must begin again, and love anew.

A.C. SWINBURNE

A Leave-Taking

Let us go hence, my songs; she will not hear.
Let us go hence together without fear;
Keep silence now, for singing-time is over,
And over all old things and all things dear.
She loves not you nor me as all we love her.
Yea, though we sang as angels in her ear,
   She would not hear.

Let us rise up and part; she will not know.
Let us go seaward as the great winds go,
Full of blown sand and foam; what help is here?
There is no help, for all these things are so,
And all the world is bitter as a tear.
And how these things are, though ye strove to show,
   She would not know.

Let us go home and hence; she will not weep.
We gave love many dreams and days to keep,
Flowers without scent, and fruits that would not grow,
Saying 'If thou wilt, thrust in thy sickle and reap.'
All is reaped now; no grass is left to mow;
And we that sowed, though all we fell on sleep,
   She would not weep.

Let us go hence and rest; she will not love,
She shall not hear us if we sing hereof,
Nor see love's ways, how sore they are and steep.
Come hence, let be, lie still; it is enough.
Love is a barren sea, bitter and deep;
And though she saw all heaven in flower above,
   She would not love.

Let us give up, go down; she will not care.
Though all the stars made gold of all the air,
And the sea moving saw before it move
One moon-flower making all the foam-flowers fair;
Though all those waves went over us, and drove
Deep down the stifling lips and drowning hair,
   She would not care.

Let us go hence, go hence; she will not see.
Sing all once more together; surely she,
She too, remembering days and words that were,
Will turn a little toward us, sighing; but we,
We are hence, we are gone, as though we had not been there.
Nay, and though all men seeing had pity on me,
   She would not see.

ARSENY TARKOVSKY

'I dreamed this dream and I still dream of it'

I dreamed this dream and I still dream of it
and I will dream of it sometime again.
Everything repeats itself and everything will be reincarnated,
and my dreams will be your dreams.

There, to one side of us, to one side of the world
wave after wave breaks on the shore:
there's a star on the wave, and a man, and a bird,
reality and dreams and death – wave after wave.

Dates are irrelevant. I was, I am, I will be.
Life is a miracle of miracles, and I kneel
before the miracle alone like an orphan,

alone in the mirrors, enclosed in reflections,
seas and towns, shining brightly through the smoke.
A mother cries and takes her baby on her knee.

Translated by Richard McKane

Nightmare of the Witch Babies

Two witch-babies,
  Ha! Ha!
Two witch-babies,
  Ho! Ho!
A bedemon-ridden hag,
  With the devil pigged alone
Begat them, laid at night
  On the bloody-rusted stone;
And they dwell within the Land
  Of the Bare Shank-Bone;
Where the Evil goes to and fro,
  Two witch babies, ho! ho! ho!

A lusty knight,
  Ha! Ha!
On a swart steed
  Ho! Ho!
Rode upon the land
  Where the silence feels alone,
Rode upon the land
  Of the Bare Shank-Bone,
Rode upon the Strand
  Of the Dead Men's Groan,
Where the Evil goes to and fro.
  Two witch-babies, ho! ho! ho!

A rotten mist,
  Ha! Ha!
Like a dead man's flesh,
  Ho! Ho!
Was abhorrent in the air,
  Clung a tether to the wood
Of the wicked looking trees,
  Was a scurf upon the flood;
And the reeds they were pulpy

With blood, blood, blood!
And the clouds were a-looming low.
    Two witch babies, ho! ho! ho!

    No one life there,
        Ha! Ha!
    No sweet life there,
        Ho! Ho!
But the long loud laugh,
    And the short shrill howl
And the quick brisk flip
    Of the hornèd owl,
As he flits right past
    With his gloomy cowl
Through the murkiness long and low.
    Two witch-babies, ho! ho! ho!

    What is it sees he?
        Ha! ha!
    There in the frightfulness?
        Ho! ho!
There he saw a maiden
    Fairest fair:
Sad were her dusk eyes,
    Long was her hair;
Sad were her dreaming eyes,
    Misty her hair,
And strange was her garments flow.
    Two witch-babies, ho! ho! ho!

    Swiftly he followed her,
        Ha! ha!
    Eagerly he followed her,
        Ho! ho!
From the rank, the greasy soil,
    Red bubbles oozed and stood;
Till it grew a putrid slime,
    And where his horse has trod,
The ground plash plashes,
    With a wet too like to blood;
And chill terrors like a fungus grow.
    Two witch-babies, ho! ho! ho!

There stood the maiden;
    Ha! ha!
Shed all her beauty,
    Ho! ho!
She shed her flower of beauty,
    Grew laidly old and dire,
Was the demon-ridden witch,
    And the consort of Hell-fire:
'Am I lovely, noble knight?
    See thy heart's own desire!
Now they come, come upon thee, lo!'
    Two witch-babies, ho! ho! ho!

Into the fogginess,
    Ha! ha!
Lo, she corrupted!
    Ho! ho!
Comes there a Death
    With the looks of a witch,
And joints that creak
    Like a night bird's scritch,
And a breath that smokes
    Like a smoking pitch,
And eyeless sockets aglow.
    Two witch-babies, ho! ho! ho!

Close behind it
    Ha! ha!
Ah! close behind it!
    Ho! ho!
Comes there a babe
    Of bloated youth,
With a curdled eye
    And a snaggy tooth,
And a life – no mortal
    Dare speak its sooth;
And its tongue like a worm doth show,
    Two witch-babies, ho! ho! ho!

Its paunch a-swollen
    Ha! ha!
Its life a-swollen

Ho! ho!
Like the [illegible] days drowned.
  Harsh was its dream
And its paunch was rent
  Like a brasten drum;
And the blubbered fat
  From its belly doth come
With a sickening ooze – Hell made it so!
  Two witch-babies, ho! ho! ho!

    It leaps on his charger,
      Ha! ha!
    It clasps him right fondly,
      Ho! ho!
Its joints are about him,
  Its breath in his bones;
Its eyes glare in his,
  And it sucks up his groans:
He falls from his horse,
  He burns on the stones,
And his mail cracks off in a glow.
  Two witch-babies, ho! ho! ho!

    Its tooth in his shoulder,
      Ha! ha!
    His skin dully champing,
      Ho! ho!
Slimed like a snail
  With that loathly thing,
His own self writhed him
  With shuddering;
His gaze grew dark
  And his soul took wing
While his breath still kept its flow.
  Two witch-babies, ho! ho! ho!

THOMAS TRAHERNE

Shadows in the Water

In unexperienc'd Infancy
Many a sweet Mistake doth ly:
Mistake tho false, intending tru;
A *Seeming* somwhat more than *View*;
    That doth instruct the Mind
    In Things that ly behind,
And many Secrets to us show
Which afterwards we com to know.

Thus did I by the Water's brink
Another World beneath me think;
And while the lofty spacious Skies
Reversed there abus'd mine Eys,
    I fancy'd other Feet
    Came mine to touch and meet;
As by som Puddle I did play
Another World within it lay.

Beneath the Water Peeple drown'd.
Yet with another Hev'n crown'd,
In spacious Regions seem'd to go
Freely moving to and fro:
    In bright and open Space
    I saw their very face;
Eys, Hands, and Feet they had like mine;
Another Sun did with them shine.

'Twas strange that Peeple there should walk,
And yet I could not hear them talk:
That throu a little watry Chink,
Which one dry Ox or Horse might drink,
    We other Worlds should see,
    Yet not admitted be;
And other Confines there behold
Of Light and Darkness, Heat and Cold.

I call'd them oft, but call'd in vain;
No Speeches we could entertain:
Yet did I there expect to find
Som other World, to pleas my Mind.
    I plainly saw by these
     A new *Antipodes*,
Whom, tho they were so plainly seen,
A Film kept off that stood between.

By walking Men's reversed Feet
I chanc'd another World to meet;
Tho it did not to View exceed
A Phantasm, 'tis a World indeed,
    Where Skies beneath us shine,
    And Earth by Art divine
Another face presents below,
Where Peeple's feet against Ours go.

Within the Regions of the Air,
Compass'd about with Hev'ns fair,
Great Tracts of Land there may be found
Enricht with Fields and fertil Ground;
    Where many num'rous Hosts,
    In those far distant Coasts,
For other great and glorious Ends,
Inhabit, my yet unknown Friends.

O ye that stand upon the Brink,
Whom I so near me, throu the chink,
With Wonder see: What Faces there,
Whose Feet, whose Bodies, do ye wear?
    I my Companions see
    In You, another Me.
They seemed Others, but are We;
Our second Selvs those Shadows be.

Look how far off those lower Skies
Extend themselvs! scarce with mine Eys
I can them reach. O ye my Friends,
What *Secret* borders on those Ends?
    Are lofty Hevens hurl'd
    'Bout your inferior World?

Are ye the Representatives
Of other Peopl's distant Lives?

Of all the Play-mates which I knew
That here I do the Image view
In other Selvs; what can it mean?
But that below the purling Stream
     Som unknown Joys there be
     Laid up in Store for me;
To which I shall, when that thin Skin
Is broken, be admitted in.

HENRY VAUGHAN

The Old Man of Verona out of Claudian

Most happy man! who in his own sweet *fields*
Spent all his time, to whom one *Cottage* yields
In *age* and *youth* a lodging: who grown *old*
Walks with his *staff* on the same *soil* and *mold*
Where he did creep an *infant*, and can tell
Many fair years spent in one quiet *Cell*!
No *toils* of fate made him from home far known,
Nor forreign *waters* drank, driv'n from his own.
No loss by *Sea*, no wild *lands* wastful war
Vex'd him; not the brib'd *Coil* of *gowns* at bar.
Exempt from *cares*, in *Cities* never seen
The fresh *field-air* he loves, and rural *green*.
The years set *turns* by *fruits*, not *Consuls* knows;
Autumn by apples: *May* by blossom'd boughs.
Within one hedge his *Sun* doth set and rise,
The world's wide day his short Demeasnes comprise.
Where he observes some known, concrescent *twig*
Now grown an *Oak*, and old, like him, and big.

Verona he doth for the *Indies* take,
And as the *red Sea* counts *Benacus* lake.
Yet are his *limbs* and *strength* untir'd, and he
A lusty *Grandsire* three *descents* doth see.
Travel and sail who will, search sea, or shore;
This man hath *liv'd*, and that hath *wander'd* more.

Peace

My Soul, there is a Countrie
    Far beyond the stars,
Where stands a winged Centrie
    All skilfull in the wars,
There above noise, and danger
    Sweet peace sits crown'd with smiles,
And one born in a Manger
    Commands the Beauteous files,
He is thy gracious friend,
    And (O my Soul awake!)
Did in pure love descend
    To die here for thy sake,
If thou canst get but thither,
    There growes the flowre of peace,
The Rose that cannot wither,
    Thy fortresse, and thy ease;
Leave then thy foolish ranges;
    For none can thee secure,
But one, who never changes,
    Thy God, thy life, thy Cure.

ANNA WICKHAM

The Fired Pot

In our town, people live in rows.
The only irregular thing in a street is the steeple;
And where that points to, God only knows,
And not the poor disciplined people!

And I have watched the women growing old,
Passionate about pins, and pence, and soap,
Till the heart beneath my wedded breast grew cold,
And I lost hope.

But a young soldier came to our town,
He spoke his mind most candidly.
He asked me quickly to lie down,
And that was very good for me.
For though I gave him no embrace –
Remembering my duty –
He altered the expression of my face,
And gave me back my beauty.

Some R&B and Black Pop

I refused to say anything
when Charlie and Inez Foxx sang 'Mockingbird',
or Oscar Wills sang 'Flat Foot Sam'.
I remained silent throughout Elmore James's version
of 'Stormy Monday'. I didn't give in
to Jerry Allison or Sonny Boy Williamson.

I broke down and admitted everything
when I reached the place on the tape
where Lazy Lester's 'I'm a Lover Not a Fighter'
suddenly gets much louder
and one of us always had to get out of bed
to turn the volume down.

Legend

X's darken the map of London
in the places we made love.
Footprints hurry back and forth
from Chelsea to Ladbroke Grove.

Winged hearts accompany our progress.
Flaming arrows signify intent.
Grappling hooks are loving glances.
Handcuffs are kindly meant.

Knives and forks are for dining out.
Wine glasses are for romancing.
Skeletons mark the Latin American clubs
where we used to go dancing.

Balcony Scene

The street light shorting on and off,
casting a balcony on my bedroom wall.
I seem to have wired it up
to my thoughts of you, your first floor studio,
the ladder to your bed, car lights overhead.

I was climbing the ladder one night
when I caught the eye of a man
going past on the top of a bus
and for one moment became him
as he turned to look back at us.
I fell asleep after that, never dreaming
I would give it a second thought.

I see his face now, passing my window,
as I draw the curtains for the night,
the street light shorting on and off,
somehow refusing to blow.

JOHN WILMOT, EARL OF ROCHESTER

Upon Nothing

Nothing! thou elder brother even to Shade:
Thou hadst a being ere the world was made,
And well fixed, art alone of ending not afraid.

Ere Time and Place were, Time and Place were not,
When primitive Nothing something straight begot;
Then all proceeded from the great united What.

Something, the general attribute of all,
Severed from thee, its sole original,
Into thy boundless self must undistinguished fall;

Yet Something did thy mighty power command,
And from thy fruitful Emptiness's hand
Snatched men, beasts, birds, fire, water, air, and land.

Matter, the wicked'st offspring of thy race,
By Form assisted, flew from thy embrace,
And rebel Light obscured thy reverend dusky face.

With Form and Matter, Time and Place did join;
Body, thy foe, with these did leagues combine
To spoil thy peaceful realm, and ruin all thy line;

But turncoat Time assists the foe in vain,
And bribed by thee, destroys their short-lived reign,
And to thy hungry womb drives back thy slaves again.

Though mysteries are barred from laic eyes,
And the Divine alone with warrant pries
Into thy bosom, where the truth in private lies,

Yet this of thee the wise may truly say:
Thou from the virtuous nothing dost delay,
And to be part of thee the wicked wisely pray.

Great Negative, how vainly would the wise
Inquire, define, distinguish, teach, devise,
Didst thou not stand to point their blind philosophies!

Is or Is Not, the two great ends of Fate,
And True or False, the subject of debate,
That perfect or destroy the vast designs of state —

When they have racked the politician's breast,
Within thy bosom most securely rest,
And when reduced to thee, are least unsafe and best.

But Nothing, why does Something still permit
That sacred monarchs should in council sit
With persons highly thought at best for nothing fit,

While weighty Something modestly abstains
From princes' coffers, and from statesmen's brains,
And Nothing there like stately Nothing reigns?

Nothing! who dwellst with fools in grave disguise,
For whom they reverend shapes and forms devise,
Lawn sleeves and furs and gowns, when they like thee look wise,

French truth, Dutch prowess, British policy,
Hibernian learning, Scotch civility,
Spaniards' dispatch, Danes' wit are mainly seen in thee;

The great man's gratitude to his best friend,
Kings' promises, whores' vows – towards thee they bend,
Flow swiftly into thee, and in thee ever end.

HENRY WOOLF

'Who taught you'

Who taught you
Contrariness,
Mazy, ambivalent
Progressions?
Or to disguise
Your watery margins
With simple rectitude
Of speech and dress?

Who knew
I would come
Lumbering after?

Parents

Incoherent reminders
Choke in his handshake
Drown in her cups of tea.

The door closes on the wrong reply.

DAVID WRIGHT

Encounter in a Glass

Skin coarse, bird-shotted nose, the flesh loose,
Almost a hammock underneath the chin;
Eyebrows en brosse – a zareba, that one –
A sprout of hair in earhole and nostril,
Lines traversing like mountain trods the forehead –
I almost wondered who the fellow was.

I knew him well enough, the non-stranger,
Yet was – as, despite a remembered face,
One can't identify some familiar
Acquaintance in an unaccustomed place –
About to make the oddest of faux pas:
To offer him my seat, and call him sir.

Winter Verses for Tambimuttu

What, in a letter to the dead,
Is better than to say what is?
Dear Tambi, as I write, the snow
Wheels slowly down, and will not stay;
And I am lost for words to say
This January afternoon.

Here is the view from my window:
Dark branches draw a skeleton
Tree against the fail of day,
And under, Eden's waters run
In stillness to the Irish sea.
They falter only at the ford

To etch a line of white across
Their moving motionless surface
As dark as the denuded boughs
That frame a glimmer in the west:
The sun that is about to die,
To burn tomorrow in the east.

I turn the leaves of memory
To see you, prince of Rathbone Place,
In blackout years, defying with
Magnanimous and careless spirit
A boring war, and holding court
In flyblown pubs for useless art;

You kept a spark alive, I think,
In that dead time, as dead as this
Midwinter landscape I look at,
Where, though the summer leaves be lost,
The living sap's in branch and root,
In ambush for a certain spring.

GREVILLE PRESS PUBLICATIONS
1975–2010

1977
George Barker, *Seven Poems*. With drawings by Richard Williams

1978
Anyte. Poems translated by John Heath-Stubbs and Carol Whiteside, with drawings by Jenny Harrison

1979
Harold Pinter, *I Know the Place*. With drawings by Michael Kenny
Poets. An anthology selected by Anthony Astbury and G.H. Godbert

1980
David Gascoyne, *Early Poems*. With drawings by Barry Burman
John Wain (trans.), *The Seafarer*. With a drawing by Brenda Stones

1981
Fulke Greville, *Poems*. Selected by Anthony Astbury with a drawing by
    David Stoker
Mary, Queen of Scots. An anthology of poetry selected and with an intro-
    duction by Antonia Fraser, with drawings by Rebecca Fraser
    [Methuen, in association with Greville Press]

1982
Emscote Anthology 1972-1982. Selected with an introduction by George
    Barker
Anne Ridler, *A Matter of Life and Death*. With a drawing by Frances
    Whistler

1983
Anthony Astbury and Geoffrey Godbert, *Still Lifes: Poems for Sydney and
    Nessie Graham*

1984
Anthony Astbury, *A Visit to Anne Frank's House*
Hartley Coleridge, *Poems*. Selected by Anthony Astbury
Roger Howard, *Ancient Rivers*. With drawings by Danny Milne

Danny Milne, *The Clouded Glass*. With drawings by the poet
Robert M. Pollet, *Poems*
Sally Purcell, *Guenever and the Looking Glass*. With drawings by William
Leaf

1985

Gillian Allnutt, *Lizzie Siddall: Her Journal (1862)*. With a drawing by
D.G. Rossetti
Anthony Astbury, *At Alderman Smith's*. With decorations by Julie
Westbury
Anthony Astbury, *Odyssey*. With maps drawn by Daniel Milne
Nessie Dunsmuir, *Nessie Dunsmuir's Seven Poems*. With a drawing by
W.S. Graham
The Emscote Book of Verse. An anthology selected by Anthony Astbury,
with drawings by children
Geoffrey H. Godbert, *The Theatre of Decision*. With drawings by Brian
Harris
Arthur Rimbaud, *The Sun was Still Warm*. Translated by Nigel Foxell
and Anthony Astbury
Gaspara Stampa. Poems translated by Sally Purcell.

1986

George Barker, *The Jubjub Bird and A Little Honouring of Lionel Johnson*
Geoffrey Godbert, *The Brooklyn Bridge*. With a photograph by William
Grantham
100 Poems by 100 Poets. An anthology selected by Harold Pinter,
Geoffrey Godbert and Anthony Astbury [Methuen, in association
with Greville Press; published in the United States by Grove Press]

1987

Liu Tao Tao (trans.), *Poems from Old China*
Roger Pringle, *The Seasons' Difference*

1988

George Barker, *Seventeen*
Nessie Dunsmuir, *Nessie Dunsmuir's Ten Poems*. With a drawing by W.S.
Graham
David Gascoyne, *Extracts from 'A Kind of Declaration' and 'Prelude to a
New Fin-de-Siècle'*. With a drawing by David Stoker
Judith Kazantzis, *A Poem for Guatemala*. With a photograph by Joe Fish
Julian Orde, *Conjurors*. With an introduction by David Wright

1989

Alison Appelbe, *Audits and Auditions*

Anthony Astbury, *My W.S. Graham Wall*. With photographs by John Cooke

Gioconda Belli, *Nicaragua Water Fire*. Translated by John Lyons

Edna O'Brien, *On the Bone*

1990

W.S. Graham, *Uncollected Poems*

Nazim Hikmet, *A Sad State of Freedom*. Translated by Taner Baybars and Richard McKane

David Wright, *Elegies*

1991

Charles Baudelaire, *Le Voyage*. Translated by Arthur Osborne

Julie Kane, *The Bartender Poems*

Marius Kociejowski, *Coast*

Poems for Shakespeare. An anthology selected by Anthony Astbury

C.H. Sisson, *Nine Sonnets*

1992

Kate Ellis, *to dine here*

Harold Pinter, *Ten Early Poems*

Arseny Tarkovsky, *Poems*. Translated by Richard McKane

1993

Anywhere Out of the World. An anthology selected by Geoffrey Godbert

Gail Dendy, *Assault and the Moth*

1994

Thomas Carew, *Love Poems*. Selected by Anthony Astbury

99 Poems in Translation. An anthology selected by Harold Pinter, Geoffrey Godbert and Anthony Astbury [Faber and Faber, in association with Greville Press; published in the United States by Grove Press]

1995

Abraham Cowley, *Love Poems*. Selected by Anthony Astbury

1996

James Elroy Flecker, *Poems*. Selected by Anthony Astbury

1997

Edward, Lord Herbert of Cherbury, *Poems*. Selected by Anthony Astbury

1998

W.S. Graham. Poems selected by Nessie Dunsmuir, with photograph by Michael Snow

George Herbert, *Poems*. Selected by Anthony Astbury

Hugo Williams, *Some R&B and Black Pop*

1999

Alex Allison, *Every Celebration*. With introduction by David Astbury

Thomas Blackburn, *For a Child*. Selected by Julia Blackburn

2000

Robert Graves, *Yesterday Only and Other Poems*. Selected by Beryl Graves

Thomas Traherne, *Poems*. Selected by Anne Ridler

2001

Robert Bridges, *Poems*. Selected by Anne Ridler

David Gascoyne, *Poems*. Selected with an introduction by Judy Gascoyne

Anne Ridler, *Poems*. Selected with a preface by Vivian Ridler

C.H. Sisson. Poems selected by Nora Sisson

Henry Vaughan, *Poems*. Selected by Anthony Astbury

2002

William Bell, *Twenty Sonnets*. Selected with an introduction by John Heath-Stubbs

John Clare, *Poems*. Selected with an introduction by Ronald Blythe

Homer, *In Cyclops' Cave*. Translated and with an illustration by Judith Kazantzis

Philip Larkin, *Poems*. Selected by Harold Pinter

John Masefield, *Poems*. Selected by Peter Vansittart

Danny Milne, *Shadows*

Harold Pinter, *Poems*. Chosen with a foreword by Antonia Fraser

Stevie Smith, *Stevie: A Motley Selection of Her Poems*. Selected by John Horder and Chris Saunders

2003

B.H. Fraser, *City Poems*

John Heath-Stubbs, *Fourteen Poems*. Selected by Anthony Astbury
Robert Herrick, *Lyrics of Love and Desire*. Edited by A.C. Grayling
Bernard Spencer, *Poems*. Selected with a note by John Press
Henry Woolf, *In the Mousetrap*
David Wright, *Poems*. Selected by Oonagh Swift

2004

George Barker, *Poems*. Selected with a foreword by Elspeth Barker
Grey Gowrie, *From Primrose Hill*
Ian Hamilton, *Fifteen Poems*. Selected and introduced by Hugo
Williams
George Herbert, *Poems*. Chosen and introduced by David Gascoyne
John Keats, *Poems*. Selected by Nigel Foxell
John Press, *Poems*. Selected by Anthony Astbury
Edward Thomas, *Poems*. Selected with a foreword by Myfanwy Thomas

2005

Lawrence Durrell, *Too Far to Hear the Singing*. Selected with a preface
by Françoise Kestman Durrell
Grey Gowrie, *Aspects of a Novel*
Grey Gowrie, *Dingle*
Grey Gowrie, *The Domino Hymn: Poems from Harefield*
Grey Gowrie, *Quartet for Charlotte*
W.S. Graham, *Fifteen Postcards*. Selected by Anthony Astbury
Angela Hall, *Winter Bride and other poems*. Selected and introduced by
Simon Gray
Libby Houston, *Tam Lin and Other Tales*
Lionel Johnson, *Love's Ways and Other Poems*. Selected by Anthony
Astbury
Robert Nye, *Sixteen Poems*. Selected by Anthony Astbury
Po Chü-I, *Poems*. Translated by Arthur Waley, selected by Anthony
Astbury
Alan Ross, *Poems*. Selected by Peter Vansittart
Elizabeth Smart, *Poems*. Selected by Sebastian Barker
The Tenth Muse: An Anthology. Edited by Anthony Astbury with a
preface by Michael Schmidt [Carcanet Press, in association with
Greville Press]
Dylan Thomas, *Poems*. Selected with an introduction by Aeronwy
Thomas

2006

Charles Baudelaire, *Poems*. Translated by Roy Campbell, selected by

Anthony Astbury

Ernest Dowson, *Some Poems*. Selected with a foreword by Robert Nye

Grey Gowrie, *For George Herbert*

Grey Gowrie, *Gardener's Tale*

Boris Pasternak, *Late Poems*. English versions by Michael Harari, selected by Anthony Astbury

Henry Reed, *The Auction Sale*. With an introduction by Jon Stallworthy

2007

Thomas Campion, *Poems*. Selected with a foreword by Grey Gowrie

Emily Dickinson, *1862*. Selected by Anthony Astbury

W.S. Graham, *Poems*. Selected by Anthony Astbury

Giacomo Leopardi, *Poems*. Translated by John Heath-Stubbs, selected by Anthony Astbury

Richard Lovelace, *Poems*. Selected by Anthony Astbury

Harold Pinter, *Six Poems for A*

Anne Ridler and Anthony Astbury (eds), *The Poetry of Praise: A Selection of Hymns*

Rainer Maria Rilke, *Requiem for Wolf Graf von Kalckreuth*. Translated by J.B. Leishman

Anna Wickham, *Poems*. Selected with a preface by Helena Nelson

2008

Guillaume Apollinaire, *Zone*. Translated with a foreword by Oliver Bernard

Doris Astbury, *Ten Drawings*. Selected by Anthony Astbury

Ian Bamford, *Paintings and Drawings*

George Barker, *Poems*. Selected by Anthony Astbury

Calling on W.S. Graham: Photographs. Selected by Anthony Astbury

Catullus, *Lesbia*. Translated by Peter Whigham, selected by Anthony Astbury

C.P. Cavafy, *Poems*. Selected by Anthony Astbury

Thomas Chatterton, *Some Poems*. Selected with a foreword by Robert Nye

Hart Crane, *Poems*. Selected by Anthony Astbury

John Donne, *Poems*. Selected with a preface by Brian Statham

T.S. Eliot, *The Love Song of J. Alfred Prufrock*

Martin Farren, *The Name of This Poem is Always the Same*

George Gascoigne, *A Packet of Poems*. Selected by Martin Farren

A.E. Housman, *Poems*. Selected with a foreword by Elspeth Barker

Walter Savage Landor, *Poems*. Selected by Jean Field

Eugene Lee-Hamilton, *Imaginary Sonnets*. Selected by Anthony Astbury

Antonio Machado, *Poem of a Day*. Translated by Charles Tomlinson
Clere Parsons, *Some Poems*. Selected with a note by Robert Nye
Fernando Pessoa, *Tobacconist's*. Translated by Jonathan Griffin
Edgar Allan Poe, *Annabel Lee and Other Poems*. Selected by Anthony
    Astbury
Ezra Pound, *Poems*. Selected with a foreword by Oliver Cox
Brian Statham, *Photographs*. Selected by Anthony Astbury
Sir John Suckling, *Love Poems*. Selected by Anthony Astbury
Richard Williams, *Paintings and Drawings*. Selected by Anthony Astbury
John Wilmot, Earl of Rochester, *Poems*. Selected by Anthony Astbury

2009

Anthony Astbury, *Two Letters to George Barker*
Norman Cameron, *Poems*. Selected with a foreword by Warren Hope
S.T. Coleridge and William Wordsworth, *Two Odes*
Sir John Davies, *Orchestra*
A Greek Garland: Poems from the Greek Anthology. Translated with a
    preface by Peter Jay
Harold Pinter, *Fourteen Poems*. Selected by Anthony Astbury
James Reeves, *Some Poems*. Selected with a foreword by Robert Nye
Martin Seymour-Smith, *The Liquid Rhinoceros and Other Uncollected
    Poems*. Edited with a foreword by Robert Nye
William Shakespeare, *Twenty Shakespeare Songs*. Selected with a fore-
    word and commentary by Roger Pringle
A.C.H. Smith, *Poems*. Selected with a foreword by Tom Stoppard
Jon Stallworthy, *War Poet*
A.C. Swinburne, *Poems*. Selected by Anthony Astbury
Francis Thompson, *Nightmare of the Witch Babies*
25 Greville Covers. Designed and printed by Peter Lloyd, selected by
    Anthony Astbury

2010

All Saints Revile Her: Twenty-one Love Poems. Selected by Anthony
    Astbury
Anthony Astbury, *Letters to Harold Pinter*
Anthony Astbury, *Letters to W.S. Graham and Nessie Dunsmuir*
Anthony Astbury, *Verse for Harold Pinter*
William Blake, *Auguries of Innocence*
Emily Brontë, *Poems*. Selected by Anthony Astbury
William Collins, *Odes*
Richard Crashaw, *A Hymn to the Name and Honour of the Admirable Saint
    Theresa*

Elizabeth Daryush, *Poems*. Selected with a preface by Michael Schmidt
Barnabe Googe, *Poems*. Selected by Anthony Astbury
Grey Gowrie, *Nursery Rhyme for Ninety*
W.S. Graham, *15 Autograph Letters*. Selected by Anthony Astbury
W.S. Graham, *Letters and Postcards to Anthony Astbury*
Thomas Hardy, *Poems*. Selected by A.C. Grayling
John Keats, *To Fanny Brawne*
Man, Dream No More of Curious Mysteries: An Anthology of Religious Poetry.
    Selected by Anthony Astbury
George Meredith, *Love in the Valley and Modern Love*
Charlotte Mew, *Poems*. Selected by Anthony Astbury
Harold Monro, *Some Poems*. Selected by Stephen Rogers
Michael Oakeshott, *The Voice of Poetry in the Conversation of Mankind*
John Oldham, *The Third Satire of Juvenal Imitated*
Petrarch, *After Laura's Death*. Translated by Mark Musa
Michael Schmidt, *Poems*
Sir Charles Sedley, *Poems*. Selected by Anthony Astbury
J.M. Synge, *Poems*. Selected by Anthony Astbury
Alfred, Lord Tennyson, *Poems*. Selected with a foreword by Elspeth
    Barker
W.B. Yeats, *Poems*. Selected by Edna O'Brien

Forthcoming
Gerard Manley Hopkins – Henry King – Thomas Lodge – John Marston –
Anthony Powell – Francis Quarles – Delmore Schwartz

INDEX OF TITLES

ACKNOWLEDGEMENTS

I would like to express my gratitude to William Baker, George Barker, Charlie Boxer, Martin Farren, Bryan Foster, Nigel Foxell, Geoffrey Godbert, Grey Gowrie, W.S. Graham, A.C. Grayling, Peter Lloyd, Robert Nye, Mark O'Connor, Harold Pinter, Chris Sheppard, Michael Schmidt and all at Carcanet, Tom Stoppard, and the Woo Foundation, without whose support this book would never have been possible.

A.A.
Warwick 2010

For permission to reprint in-copyright material, grateful acknowledgement is made as follows:

ALEX ALLISON, 'Olive Tree', from *Every Celebration* (Greville Press, 1998), first published by the Manchester Institute of Contemporary Arts, 1967. Copyright © the Estate of Alex Allison. GILLIAN ALLNUTT, 'Laudanum' and 'I, Lizzie, once a girl' from 'Lizzie Siddall: Her Journal (1862)', from Gillian Allnutt, *How the Bicycle Shone: New and Selected Poems* (Bloodaxe Books, 2007).Copyright © Gillian Allnutt, included by permission of the publisher. ANYTE, 'On a Dolphin', 'Many times lamenting, Cleina, the mother' and 'In life this man was Manes, a slave', trans. Carol Whiteside and John Heath-Stubbs, from *Anyte*, translated from the Greek by Carol Whiteside and John Heath-Stubbs (Greville Press, 1979). Copyright © the Estate of Carol Whiteside and the Estate of John Heath-Stubbs, included by permission of David Higham Associates. GUILLAUME APOLLINAIRE, 'Zone', is taken from *Guillaume Apollinaire: Selected Poems,* translated by Oliver Bernard. Published by Anvil Press Poetry in 1986. New edition 2004. Included by permission of the publisher. ALISON APPLEBE, 'Woman', 'Gargoyle' and 'Sex Objects', from *Audits and Ambitions* (Greville Press, 1989). Copyright © Alison Applebe, included by permission of the author. ANTHONY ASTBURY, 'Letter', 'Warwick', 'Loss' and 'English Lesson', from *Selected Verse* (Ashby Lane Press, 2009). Copyright © Anthony Astbury. GEORGE BARKER, 'Roman Poem III' and 'Morning in Norfolk', from *Selected Poems* (Faber and Faber, 1995). Copyright © the Estate of George Barker, included by permission of the publisher and the Estate of George Barker. CHARLES BAUDELAIRE, 'The Voyage', trans. Arthur Osborne, from Charles Baudelaire, *Le Voyage*, translated by Arthur Osborne (Greville Press, 1991). Copyright © the Estate of Arthur Osborne. WILLIAM BELL, 'All summer long in dreams I would remember' and 'Perhaps the unbroken colt beside the river', from *Mountains Beneath the Horizon* (Faber and Faber, 1950). Copyright © the Estate of William Bell, included by permission of the publisher. GIACONDA BELLI, 'New York' trans. John Lyons, from *Nicaragua Water Fire* (Greville Press, 1989). Copyright © Giaconda Belli, 1989. Used by permission of the author. Translation copyright © John Lyons, included by permission of the translator. THOMAS BLACKBURN, 'The Unpredictable' and 'An Epitaph', from *Selected Poems* (Carcanet Press, 2001). Copyright © the Estate of Thomas Blackburn, included by permission of the Estate and the publisher. NORMAN CAMERON, 'A Visit to the Dead', is taken from Norman Cameron: *Collected Poems and Selected Translations,* edited by Warren Hope and Jonathan Barker, published by Anvil Press Poetry in 1990. Copyright © the Estate of Norman Cameron, included by permission of the Estate and the publisher. CATULLUS, 'Lesbia' from *The Poems of Catullus*, translated with an introduction by Peter Whigham (Penguin Classics, 1966). Copyright © Penguin Books Ltd, 1966. JOHN CLARE, 'The Gipsy Camp', from *John Clare*, selected and edited by R.K.R. Thornton (J.M. Dent, Everyman, 1979). ELIZABETH DARYUSH, 'Autumn, dark wanderer halted here once more', 'Anger lay by me all night long' and 'Still-Life', copyright © Carcanet Press Ltd., included by permission of Carcanet Press. GAIL DENDY, 'The Coin of Africa', 'Assault' and 'Goodbye and All That', from *Assault and the Moth* (Greville Press, 1993). Copyright © Gail Dendy, included by permission of the author. NESSIE DUNSMUIR, 'I would have chosen children' and 'He for whose sake', copyright © Literary Estate of Nessie Graham, included by permission of the Literary Estate. LAWRENCE DURRELL, 'Nobody', copyright © Lawrence Durrell 1971; 'A Patch of Dust', copyright © Lawrence Durrell 1974. Reproduced with permission of Faber and Faber Ltd and Curtis Brown Group Ltd, London on behalf of the Estate of Lawrence Durrell. KATE ELLIS, 'festivals of mouthpieces', from *to dine here* (Greville Press, 1992). Copyright © Kate Ellis, included by permission of the author. MARTIN FARREN, '– all that concrete, steel', from *The Name of This Poem Is Always the Same* (Greville Press, 2008). Copyright © Martin Farren, included by permission of the author. B.H. FRASER, 'Business Centre', from *City Poems* (Greville Press, 2003). Copyright © B.H. Fraser, included by permission of the author. DAVID GASCOYNE, 'The cold renunciatory beauty' and 'A Tough Generation', from *Selected Poems* (Enitharmon Press, 1994). Copyright © the Estate of David Gascoyne, included by permission of the publisher and the Estate of David Gascoyne. GEOFFREY GODBERT, 'Of course you are beautiful', from *Collected Poems* by Geoffrey Godbert (Poetry Monthly Press, 2007). Copyright © Geoffrey Godbert, included by permission of the author. GREY GOWRIE, 'From Primrose Hill', from *Third Day* (Carcanet Press, 2008). Copyright © Grey Gowrie, included by permission of the publisher. W.S. GRAHAM, 'Letter VI', 'The Beast in the Space' and 'Greenock at Night I Find You', from *Collected Poems* (Faber and Faber, 1979), copyright © Literary Estate of W.S. Graham, included by permission of the Literary Estate. ROBERT GRAVES, 'Despite and Still', 'What We Did Next' and 'Ouzo Unclouded', from *Complete Poems* (Carcanet Press, 1995, 1997, 1999), copyright © by the Trustees of the Robert Graves Copyright Trust, included by permission of the publisher. ANGELA HALL, 'She Always Sang' from *Winter Bride and Other Poems* (Greville Press, 2005). Copyright © Angela Hall, included by permission of the author. IAN HAMILTON, 'Almost Nothing', 'Biography' and 'Rose', from *Collected Poems, edited with an introduction by Alan Jenkins* (Faber and Faber Ltd, 2009). Copyright © the Estate of Ian Hamilton, included courtesy of the Estate of Ian Hamilton and by permission of the publisher. JOHN HEATH-STUBBS, 'Prayer to Saint Lucy', 'The Green Man's Last Will and Testament' and 'Quatrains', from *Collected Poems 1943-1987* (Carcanet Press, 1988). Copyright © the Estate of John Heath-Stubbs, included by permission of David Higham Associates and the publisher. NAZIM HIKMET, 'Advice for Someone Going into Prison', trans. Richard McKane is taken from *Nâzım Hikmet: Beyond the Walls, Selected Poems*, translated by Ruth Christie, Richard McKane and Talât Sait Halman. Published by Anvil Press Poetry in 1993. Included by permission of the publisher. LIBBY HOUSTON, 'The Story of Arachne', from *Tam Lin and Other Tales* (Greville Press, 2005). Copyright © Libby Houston, included by permission of the author. JULIE KANE, 'Kissing the Bartender', from *Rythm and Booze*. Copyright © 2003 by Julie Kane. Used with permission of the poet and the University of Illinois Press. JUDITH KAZANTZIS, 'The Dump', from *A Poem for Guatemala* (Greville Press, 1988), first published in a limited edition by Bedlam Press, 1966. Copyright © Judith Kazantzis, included by permission of the author. MARIUS KOCIEJOWSKI, 'The Water Clock' and 'Babel' are taken from *Doctor Honoris Causa* by Marius Kociejowski, published by Anvil Press Poetry in 1993. Included by permission of the publisher. GIACOMO LEOPARDI, 'The Infinite', trans. John Heath-Stubbs, from *Collected Poems 1943-1987* (Carcanet Press, 1988). Copyright © the Estate of John Heath-Stubbs, included by permission of David Higham Associates and the publisher. ANTONIO MACHADO, 'Poem of a Day', trans. Charles Tomlinson, copyright © Charles Tomlinson, included by permission of the translator. JOHN MASEFIELD, from *Reynard the Fox*, edited with an introduction by Philip W. Errington (Carcanet Press, 2008). Copyright © the Estate of John Masefield, included by permission of The Society of Authors as the literary representative of the Estate of John Masefield. DANNY MILNE, 'Abandonment', from *Shadows* (Greville Press, 2002). Copyright © Danny Milne. ROBERT NYE, 'Eurynome' from *Collected Poems* (Sinclair-Stevenson, 1995). Copyright © Robert Nye, included by permission of the author and Carcanet Press; 'Not Looking', from *The Rain and the Glass: 99 Poems, New & Selected* (Greenwich Exchange, 2004). Copyright © Robert Nye, included by permission of the author. EDNA O' BRIEN, from *On the Bone* (Greville Press, 1989). Copyright © Edna O'Brien, included by permission of the author. JULIAN ORDE, from *Conjurors* (Greville Press, 1988). Copyright © Emily Abercrombie. BORIS PASTERNAK, 'Unique Days' and 'Bread', from *Poems 1955-1959* by Boris Pasternak, translated by Michael Harari, published by Harvill Press. Reprinted by permission of The Random House Group Ltd. FERNANDO PESSOA, 'Tobacconist's', trans. Jonathan Griffin, from *Fernando Pessoa: Selected Poems*, translated by Jonathan Griffin (Penguin Books, 1974, second edition 1982). Copyright © L.M. Rosa, 1974. Introduction and trans-lation copyright © Jonathon Griffin, 1974, 1982. HAROLD PINTER, 'The Irish Shape' 'I know the place' and 'Cancer Cells', from *Collected Poems and Prose* (Faber and Faber, 1991). Copyright © the Estate of Harold Pinter, included by permission of the publisher. In the United States: 'The Irish Shape', 'Later', 'I know the place' from *Various Voices* by Harold Pinter, copyright © 1998 by Harold Pinter. Used by permis-sion of Grove/Atlantic, Inc.; 'Cancer Cells' from *The Essential Pinter* by Harold Pinter, Copyright © 2002 by Harold Pinter. Used by permission of Grove/Atlantic, Inc. PO CHÜ-I, 'Song and Dance' and 'The Chrysanthemums in the Eastern Garden', trans. Arthur Waley, from *Chinese Poems by Arthur Waley* (George Allen and Unwin, Ltd, 1946) and *The Life and Times of Po Chü-I, 772-846 AD* (George Allen and Unwin Ltd, 1949) by Arthur Waley. Copyright © by permission of the Estate of Arthur Waley, included by kind permission of The Arthur Waley Estate. ROBERT M. POLLET, 'Egyptian Child', from *Poems* (Greville Press, 1984). Copyright © the Estate of Robert Pollet, included by permission of the Estate of Robert Pollet. JOHN PRESS, 'Womanisers' and 'The Shadows', from *Poems* (Greville Press, 2004). Copyright © the Estate of John Press. ROGER PRINGLE, 'Neighbours', from *The Season's Difference* (Greville Press, 1987). Copyright © Roger

Pringle. SALLY PURCELL, 'Guenever and the looking-glass' and 'March 1603' are taken from Sally Purcell: *Collected Poems*, edited by Peter Jay, published by Anvil Press Poetry in 2002. Included by permission of the publisher. HENRY REED, 'The Auction Sale', from *Collected Poems* (Carcanet Press, 2007). Copyright © the Executor of the Estate of Henry Reed, included by permission of the publisher. JAMES REEVES, 'The Little Brother' and 'The Prisoners', from *Collected Poems 1929-1974* (Heinemann, 1974). Copyright © the Estate of James Reeves. ANNE RIDLER, 'A Matter of Life and Death', from *Collected Poems* (Carcanet Press, 2004, 2007). Copyright © the Estate of Anne Ridler, included by permission of the publisher. ALAN ROSS, 'Angel of Harwich', 'Clothes on a Chair' and 'Leave Train', from *Poems* (Greville Press, 2005). Copyright © the Estate of Alan Ross, included by permission of the Estate of Alan Ross. MARTIN SEYMOUR-SMITH, 'On the Beach' and 'Learning to Fall Out of Love', from *The Liquid Rhinoceros and other uncollected poems* (Greville Press, 2009). Copyright © Martin Seymour-Smith, reprinted with permission of Miranda and Charlotte Seymour-Smith. C.H. SISSON, 'If love and death are one and the same thing', 'For the Queen's Jubilee' and 'Ellick Farm' from *Collected Poems* (Carcanet Press, 1998).Copyright © the Estate of C.H. Sisson, included by permission of the publisher. ELIZABETH SMART, 'Slightly Rhyming Verses For Jeff Bernard's Fiftieth Birthday', from *Poems* (Greville Press, 2005). Copyright © the Estate of Elizabeth Smart, included by permission of the Estate of Elizabeth Smart. A.C.H. SMITH, 'Structures of Cancer', from *Poems* (Greville Press, 2009). Copyright © 2009 A.C.H. Smith. STEVIE SMITH, 'To Carry the Child', from *Collected Poems* (Penguin Books, 1975). Copyright © the Estate of Stevie Smith, included by permission of the Estate of James MacGibbon. BERNARD SPENCER, 'On the 'Sievering' Tram' and 'Part of Plenty', from Poems (Greville Press, 2003). Copyright © the Estate of Bernard Spencer. JON STALLWORTHY, 'War Poet' (Greville Press, 2009). Copyright © Jon Stallworthy, included by permission of the author. GASPARA STAMPA, 'Love, standing by my side' and 'All the planets in heaven, all the stars', trans. Sally Purcell, from *Gaspara Stampa*, translated by Sally Purcell (Greville Press, 1984). Copyright © the Estate of Sally Purcell. ARSENY TARKOVSKY, 'I dreamed this dream and I still dream of it', trans. Richard McKane, from *Arseny Tarkovsky: Poems* (Greville press, 1992). Copyright © the Estate of Arseny Tarkovsky. Translation copyright © Richard McKane. Included by permission of Marina Tarkovskaya and Richard McKane. ANNA WICKHAM, 'The Fired Pot', from *Poems* (Greville Press, 2007). Copyright © the Estate of Anna Wickham, included by permission of

George Hepburn and Margaret Hepburn. HUGO WILLIAMS, 'Some R&B and Black Pop', 'Legend' and 'Balcony Scene', from *Collected Poems* (Faber and Faber Ltd, 2002). Copyright © Hugo Williams, included by permission of the publisher. HENRY WOOLF, 'Who taught you' and 'Parents', from *In the Mousetrap* (Greville Press, 2003). Copyright © Henry Woolf., included by permission of the author. DAVID WRIGHT, 'Encounter in a Glass' and 'Winter Verses for Tambimuttu', from *Poems and Versions* (Carcanet Press, 1992). Copyright © the Estate of David Wright, included by permission of the publisher.

Every effort has been made to trace copyright holders. The editor and publisher apologise if any material has been included without appropriate acknowledgement, and would be glad to correct any errors or omissions in future editions.